A Place
of Their Own

A Place
of Their Own

Creating the Deaf Community in America

JOHN VICKREY VAN CLEVE
BARRY A. CROUCH

Gallaudet University Press
Washington, D.C.

Gallaudet University Press, Washington, D.C. 20002

© 1989 by Gallaudet University. All rights reserved

Published 1989

Printed in the United States of America

08 07   9 8

Library of Congress Cataloging-in-Publication Data

Van Cleve, John V.

   A place of their own: creating the deaf community in America /
John Vickrey Van Cleve, Barry A. Crouch.

        p.   cm.

   Bibliography: p.

   Includes index.

   ISBN 0-930323-49-1

   1. Deaf—Education—History. I. Crouch, Barry A., 1941-
II. Title.

   HV2530.V36   1989

   305.9'08162'0973—dc19   88-26996

                                                          CIP

Photograph on page 53 courtesy of the North Dakota School for the Deaf.
All other photographs courtesy of the Gallaudet University Archives.

⊗ The paper used in this publication meets the minimum requirements of
American National Standard for Information Sciences—Permanence of Paper for
Printed Library materials, ANSI Z39.48-1984.

Contents

Preface

This study grew out of a pedagogical need. In 1985 we began designing a course called the "History of the American Deaf Community," to be offered for the first time in the fall of 1986 at Gallaudet University. That such a course was only then being developed seems ironic in retrospect. Gallaudet University was more than one hundred years old; the first permanent school for deaf students had opened more than one hundred and fifty years earlier; and the American deaf community had formally established its first national organization more than ten decades earlier. The 1960s had seen a proliferation of courses in colleges, universities, and even secondary schools celebrating the history of various other American minorities, ethnic and religious groups, and women. Yet in the late 1980s Gallaudet University still did not offer a course that would help its students understand their past.

One reason was the lack of the solid historical research upon which any rigorous course must be constructed. With the exception of Jack Gannon, author of *Deaf Heritage*, deaf people had neither produced their own histories themselves nor attracted the attention of hearing scholars. Deafness for too long had been viewed from the perspective of pathology. In this view, deaf people are diseased or disabled—they lack the attributes of full humanity; therefore, the proper role of the scholar is not to understand deaf people's past for what it might reveal about the human condition but instead to find a cure, a way to make this lamentable condition—and the people who suffer from it—disappear. What could be interesting or important, after all—scholars apparently assumed—about the one in one thousand or one in two thousand people who lacked a primary sensory modality?

The absence of historical studies about deaf people also was due to characteristics that deaf people share with other minorities in American history. They usually have been poor, blocked by their hearing loss from the usual avenues to wealth in this society, and they have never held positions of political strength or importance because of their poverty and their small numbers. Thus their history was, and is, devalued. Those who control society write its past and attract the attention of its historians. We realized, then, that our first objective was to uncover what we could about the experience of a people who seemingly blend into society and leave no trace when they are gone.

Our early efforts concentrated on finding the documents that would tell us, and our students, how it was that deaf people in the United States had created a language and a community that had persisted for two centuries. When we found sources that helped to elucidate deaf Americans' murky past, we put them together into a reader, a collection of original documents. Although not completely satisfying, for only the deaf elite—those who were educated and literate—left behind written records, we hoped that this would form the basic reading material of our course and at least provide a beginning for deeper historical study.

It failed. Documents collected from sources up and down the East Coast, from Duke University to the archives of the American School for the Deaf, were simply too opaque for undergraduate students untrained in documentary analysis. They caught glimpses of their past, to be sure, but its outlines, the flow of events, personalities, and ideas that bound the deaf community into something more than a group of disparate individuals, did not take form in the students' minds. This narrative is our attempt to overcome that problem and to provide a coherent look at some aspects of the process whereby deaf Americans became the American deaf community.

The process began long before Europeans arrived on the shores of North America. The first chapter includes a brief overview of the intellectual currents that provided a basis for understanding deafness before the age of Enlightenment. The penultimate chapter concludes with the early years of the twentieth century, and the last chapter, or epilogue, provides an overview and a taste of things to come as deaf people continue to define their place within American history.

The bulk of the text, however, concerns itself with the nineteenth century. It was during this one hundred years that a revolution in the lives of deaf Americans occurred, when deaf people forged themselves into something more than a collection of individuals. For the first time, they confronted the hearing world with the strength of an organized group, and they developed strategies to cope with the unique situation in which they found themselves. As one of their leaders, Olof Hanson, wrote in the late nineteenth century, deaf people were "foreigners among a people whose language they [could] never learn."

Despite Hanson's comment, this is not a story of failure but one of success. The striking thing to us is what deaf people accomplished; the insight and realism that guided their search for full and rewarding lives stands in stark contrast to the usual picture of the pitiable deaf-mute, forever alone and incapable of communicating with other humans. Some deaf Americans have been isolated and deprived of the rewards of social intercourse, but most have not. Certainly, the deaf individuals whose history we have been able to discover do not fit the popular conception. Our goal with this text, then, has been to bring this historical reality out into the open where it can be understood and examined by hearing and deaf people alike.

Acknowledgments

Many individuals contributed to the completion of this work. Archivists were especially important. Donna Wells and David de Lorenzo, respectively the current and former head archivist at Gallaudet University, made available to us their expertise and facilities. Michael Olson, a member of the American deaf community and a Gallaudet archivist, enthusiastically assisted in locating and identifying sources in Gallaudet's vast collection of rare books, periodicals, and manuscripts. Corrine Hilton, curator of photographs at the Gallaudet University Archives, found suitable illustrations to accompany our written text. Every photograph in this book owes its existence to her skill and effort. We also wish to thank the archival staffs of the William R. Perkins Library, Duke University; the Dukes County Historical Society on Martha's Vineyard; the Massachusetts Historical Society; the Connecticut Historical Society and the Connecticut State Library, both in Hartford; the Beinecke Rare Book and Manuscript Library and the Sterling Memorial Library at Yale University; the Volta Bureau, Washington, D.C.; the Virginia State Library and the Valentine Museum, both in Richmond; and the Manuscript Division of the Library of Congress. Winfield McChord, Jr., Executive Director of the American School for the Deaf in Hartford, is not an archivist, but he enthusiastically opened to us the archival records of the excellent and venerable institution he heads.

In addition to archivists, we profited from the advice (and often trenchant criticism) of several knowledgeable persons who read drafts of the manuscript. Harlan Lane of Northeastern University and John S. Schuchman and Kathleen Shaver Arnos of Gallaudet University made particularly helpful and insightful suggestions that improved the accuracy and interpretive sophistication of the final draft.

Gallaudet University's administration and faculty committees assisted as well. Two presidential awards provided crucial financial support for travel to research collections. A sabbatical leave granted to one of the authors in the fall of 1987 was essential to finishing the book in timely fashion.

Other individuals gave support and encouragement in a variety of ways. Among these the authors wish especially to thank Larry Madaras. Our students at Gallaudet University, though too numerous to list by name, were important both in demonstrating the need for a work of this sort and in cheering us on to its completion. We owe a special debt to Jack Gannon whose pioneering study, *Deaf Heritage: A Narrative History of Deaf America*, demonstrated the value of further study of America's deaf minority. Gannon's work and Lane's monumental *When the Mind Hears: A History of the Deaf* are indispensable starting points for any serious examination of deaf Americans' past.

Finally we are grateful to Elaine Costello and Ivey Pittle of Gallaudet University Press. They expedited the production of this book, seeing it through from rough manuscript to finished product in a remarkably short time.

JVVC

BAC

1

Prophets and Physicians

In 1779 a deaf Frenchman named Pierre Desloges briefly described a vibrant Parisian deaf community, a society in which deaf individuals regularly interacted, shared a common sign language, and learned from one another.[1] Presumably this community had developed naturally from deaf peoples' need to be with each other. Large and cosmopolitan, Paris could have provided in a common location sufficient numbers of deaf residents for a deaf community to arise. Yet Paris seems to have been unique. There is no convincing evidence that deaf communities existed elsewhere until the late eighteenth and early nineteenth centuries.

Surely deaf communities did not exist in the United States. The only known concentration of deaf people was on Martha's Vineyard, and there the deaf and hearing citizens were so integrated that deaf people did not form a community apart from their hearing fellows. Both the hearing and the deaf persons used sign language, and deaf individuals usually chose hearing persons for spouses.[2] Generally, then, it seems that deaf people came together and created distinct cultural units—communities—only in response to particular historical developments of the late eighteenth and the nineteenth centuries, especially the growth of cities and the establishment of state-supported residential schools exclusively for deaf students. Yet long before deaf Americans began to form their unique community, deafness and deaf people were subjects of Western thought and literature. In the distant past, deaf people appear most often in medical and religious texts. Both the Old Testament and the New Testament of the Bible, for example, contain significant references to deaf people.

THE JUDEO-CHRISTIAN HERITAGE

Biblical discussions of deafness are not consistent. The Old Testament and the New Testament present sharply contrasting messages about deaf people. The overall attitude of the Old Testament passages is optimistic, empathetic, and positive—deaf people are not to be cursed, damned, or shunted aside; they are to be treated with the respect due to all manifestations of the divine plan. Thus in Exodus, chapter 4, the following dialogue between the Lord and Moses occurs when Moses complains that he does not speak well:

> 10 And Moses said unto the Lord, O my Lord, I am not eloquent, neither heretofore, nor since thou hast spoken unto they servant: but I am slow of speech, and of a slow tongue.[3]
>
> 11 And the Lord said unto him, Who hath made man's mouth? or who maketh the dumb, or deaf, or the seeing, or the blind? have not I the LORD?
>
> 12 Now therefore go, and I will be with thy mouth, and teach thee what thou shalt say.[3]

The passages state, unequivocally, that some people are deaf because the Lord made them that way. It implies that people should not complain or be concerned about their condition, for whatever that condition is—dumb, deaf, seeing, blind, or slow of speech like Moses—it is what God has chosen. The Lord tells Moses not to worry about his limitations, to go on with the task set for him, which may be interpreted as a command to others, also, to remember that God is with them and will help them overcome their perceived shortcomings.

The Old Testament's emphasis on respect for persons with disabilities continues in Leviticus. There, in chapter 19, verse 14, the Lord states various laws to Moses. Among them is the following: "Thou shalt not curse the deaf, nor put a stumblingblock before the blind, but shalt fear thy God: I am the LORD."

The promise of a life free from deafness and all limitations on human fulfillment appears in the Old Testament book of Isaiah. Chapter 29, verse 18, says that the day will come when "the deaf hear the words of the book." A joyful future for the people of Israel is predicted in chapter 35. Isaiah prophesies that the lame will leap like deer, the dumb will sing, streams will flow in the desert, the blind will see, and "the ears of the deaf shall be unstopped." This optimistic mood, however, is not continued in the Christians' addition to the Bible.

The New Testament contains neither commandments to treat deaf people decently nor promises that one day all shall be free of disabilities. Instead, in chapter 11 of Matthew and chapter 7 of Mark deafness is used as a means of demonstrating Jesus's ability to create miracles, to accomplish things that are impossible for humans. Mark says that a deaf person with a speech impediment was brought to Jesus:

> 33 And [Jesus] took him aside from the multitude, and put his fingers into his ears, and he spit, and touched his tongue;
>
> 34 And looking up to heaven, he sighed, and saith unto him, "Eph'pha-tha," that is, Be opened.
>
> 35 And straightway his ears were opened, and the string of his tongue was loosed, and he spake plain.
>
> 36 And he charge them that they should tell no man: but the more he charged them, so much the more a great deal they published it;
>
> 37 And were beyond measure astonished, saying, he hath done all things well: he maketh both the deaf to hear, and the dumb to speak.

Here, in the New Testament, deaf people are reduced to objects, or at best they are depicted as sick beings to be cured by the miraculous powers of Jesus. The deaf individual is lost as a human being. Mark shows no concern or empathy for the deaf man; he merely exploits his condition to demonstrate supernatural power. The possibility that deaf persons may be part of God's plan, that He created them for a larger purpose, is absent.

Some passages of the New Testament actually created problems for deaf people. The Old Testament book of Exodus had reminded the people of Israel that deaf people were part of the Lord's creation and therefore deserving of respect, but both Mark and Luke took an opposite approach. They portray deafness as an indication that an individual has been possessed by a demonic, evil being. Chapter 9 of Mark is specific about this. Mark relates that an individual brought his deaf son to Jesus. The boy had "a dumb spirit" that caused him to gnash his teeth, to foam at the mouth, and to grieve. Jesus then "rebuked the foul spirit, saying unto him, 'thou dumb and deaf spirit, I charge thee, come out of him, and enter no more into him.'" With this, the boy apparently was cured, but deaf people now could be viewed as persons somehow inhabited by an evil presence. This is a remarkable turnabout from the Old Testament view that certain people were deaf because God made them that way.

The most damaging blow to deaf people in the New Testament, however, is in a single sentence of Paul's epistle to the Romans (chapter 10, verse 17): "So then faith *cometh* by hearing, and hearing by the word of God." Whatever Paul may have meant by this, people who interpreted the Bible literally believed that it indicated that those who are deaf are denied the possibility of faith. Without faith, they cannot be Christians and cannot be saved.

CATHOLIC TRADITION

The view that deaf people cannot be Christians held sway within the Catholic church for many centuries, and it often was attributed to Saint Augustine (354–430), one of the people most responsible for defining Catholic church—and hence Christian—doctrine before the Protestant Reformation. Various commentators on Augustine stated that it was his belief that deaf people, because they cannot hear the word of God, are denied the possibility of religious salvation.[4] Augustine's attitude toward deaf people was actually somewhat different, however.

Augustine mentioned deaf persons in several places; two were particularly significant. First, in reference to Saint Paul's epistle to the Romans, Augustine wrote that deafness "is a hinderance to faith," meaning that lack of hearing makes it difficult for a person to acquire faith, not that faith is impossible for a person who cannot hear. Given the fact that no means of educating deaf people was known in Augustine's time, and given that there were no interpreters to convey Christian beliefs to deaf people, Augustine's statement seems to be a logical conclusion.[5]

Augustine's more optimistic evaluation of deaf people, and one that is remarkable for its insight and its prediction that a deaf community could exist, is in a dialogue from chapter 18 of *De quantitate animae liber unus*. In this discussion Augustine points out that he believes that deaf people can learn and thus are able to receive faith and salvation. This passage from Augustine also is revealing because it shows that, as early as the fourth century of the modern era, sign language (Augustine refers to "bodily movements," "signs," and "gestures") was used by some deaf people and that it was believed to be capable of transmitting human thought and belief. Indeed, Augustine implies that it is equal to spoken language in its ability to reach the "soul." In the dialogue, quoted below, he asks, "What does it matter" whether a person signs or speaks, "since both these pertain to the soul?"

Evodius.—It occurs to me that we should consider how it is that an infant child does not speak, but nevertheless, as he grows, acquires the faculty of speech.

Augustine.—That is an easy one; for I believe it is evident to you that every one speaks that language which is spoken by those among whom he is born and brought up.

Evodius.—Everybody knows that.

Augustine.—Imagine, then, one born and brought up in a place where men do not speak, but rather by nods and by the movement of their limbs convey to one another the thoughts which they wish to express; do you not think that he will do likewise, and that, hearing nobody speak, he also will not speak?

Evodius.—Do not ask me that, for the case is an impossible one. For who are such men, that I should imagine one to be born among them?

Augustine.—Have you not then seen at Milan a youth most fair in form and most courteous in demeanor, who yet was dumb and deaf to such a degree that he could neither understand others nor communicate what he himself desired except by means of bodily movements?

For this man is very well known. And I myself know a certain peasant, a speaking man, who by a speaking wife had four or more sons and daughters . . . who were deaf-mutes. They were perceived to be mutes, because they could not speak; and to be deaf also, because they understood only signs that could be perceived by the eye.

Evodius.—The first man I know well, and while I do not know the others, I believe what you say about them; but what are you driving at?

Augustine.—You said you could not imagine one being born among such men.

Evodius.—And I say so still; for unless I am mistaken, you admit that the persons to whom you refer were born among speaking people.

Augustine.—I do not deny it; but as we are now agreed that such men do exist, I ask you to consider this question: If a man and a woman of this kind were united in marriage and for any reason were transferred to some solitary place, where, however, they might be able to live, if they should have a son who was not deaf, how would the latter speak with his parents?

Evodius.—How can you think that he would do otherwise than reply by gestures to the signs which his parents made to him? However, a small boy could not do even this; therefore my reasoning remains sound. *For what does it matter, as he grows up, whether he speaks or makes gestures, since both these pertain to the soul?*[6]

Western religious tradition contained varied, even conflicting, attitudes toward deafness. The Judaic heritage in the Old Testament appeared to stress the importance of tolerance toward deaf people, insisting that they, like others, were God's children. The New Testament raised two frightening possibilities: that deafness was caused by an evil spirit and that deaf people could not be Christians. Catholic writers, quoting Augustine, often accepted the latter interpretation as official doctrine, ironically ignoring Augustine's perceptive and optimistic comments on the possibility of learning through sign language. The person wishing to understand deaf people and deafness, then, could learn little from the pre-Reformation church, and even less from contemporary physicians.

PHYSICIANS' VIEWS

To physicians in ancient and medieval Western societies, and perhaps to physicians today, the idea of a deaf community was absurd. To them, deafness was a malady, a physical condition that should be eliminated to allow the patient to live a healthy life. This required a cure, and physicians often prescribed solutions that they believed would be successful. One of these involved making loud noises next to the ears of the deaf individual. Despite the obvious failure of this method, it was tried repeatedly and written about in medical texts.

A sixth-century physician, Alexander of Tralles, described noise therapy in a discussion of the medical treatments for deafness of his day. Although he was not confident that physicians would be successful using any method known, he recommended that they "leave nothing undone" anyway. He wrote:

> Many doctors have not merely prescribed all possible internal methods, but, after having carried out arteriotomy [cutting of a vein to bleed the patient], take out a trumpet, place the end in the ear and blow. Others have rung large bells and yet others have used instruments of their own devising. For if in serious cases most of the remedies seem to have no worthwhile effect, one must all the same give serious thought to these and should not delay in giving help and leave nothing undone: for quite often something may occur contrary to expectation.[7]

Blowing a trumpet in someone's ear probably produced pain and may have destroyed any hearing a deaf individual previously had. Nevertheless, this practice continued at least into the seventeenth century, when it was reported that doctors in Spain put so much noise into deaf peoples' ears that the ears bled.

Ears were not only overloaded with noise; they also received substances of various kinds. Physicians frequently recommended pouring or syringing various liquids into deaf individuals' ear canals. Medieval texts mentioned oil, honey, vinegar, bile of rabbits or pigs, garlic juice, human milk, smoked goat's urine, and eel fat mixed with blood as auditory canal purgatives. The rationale for these concoctions presumably was that they would open the pathways connecting the brain, or inner hearing mechanism, with outside noise. Although incorrect, this explanation contains some common-sensical notions.[8]

By contrast, the following passage from a Venetian medical text of 1557, which attempted to clarify the reasons for a boy's deafness, shows just how muddled thinking about deafness was:

> Nikolaus . . . was five years old [when] he caught a strong fever so that doctors gave him up for lost. However, his godmother tried all sorts of medicines and, among other things, also laid portions of the disembowelled carcasses of young dogs on his head. Perhaps because of this or some lucky chance the boy was cured of his fever in eight days but as a result became more seriously ill so that his arms and legs, especially the left side, were paralyzed. Moreover the boy, who previously was able to speak and hear, lost his hearing so that he could have been thought dumb. The fever began on the 15th July and, as we have said lasted eight days. The paralysis however remained throughout the winter until April so that in May the boy was completely cured of the paralysis but could still neither hear nor speak.
>
> We must however assume that the head of the boy, whose humour was wet, was also wet and filled with waste matter and that, due to the fever and the warmth of the dogs' carcasses on his head, this seeped through to his cranium so that this thick slime, by discharging onto the nerval bases, caused obstruction of the nerval canals in the weakened and infirmed body. After this obstruction occurred and the life force was prevented from passing through the nerves, by which the motive impulses reached the muscles, then paralysis or loosening of the limbs occurred. Since not merely the nerves which assist movement, were obstructed by the cold wet slime, but also those which conduct the hearing functions and speech, the boy became not only hard-of-hearing but completely deaf and dumb.[9]

Passages such as this were becoming anomalous by the late sixteenth century; in 1591 Solomon Alberti, a German physician, published the first book of any kind specifically about deafness, *Discourse on Deafness and Speechlessness*. Alberti became the first physician to state unequivocally that hearing and speech were separate functions. He argued from anatomical study of cadavers that the nerves controlling speech and hearing entered the brain in different places and were not connected. More importantly, Alberti wrote that deaf people were rational and capable of thought, even though they lacked speech. He stated that he knew a deaf person who could read, and he claimed to have met deaf people who could understand speech by observing the movements of the lips.[10]

Alberti was part of a sudden awakening of interest in deafness. In the same year in which his *Discourse on Deafness and Speechlessness* appeared, another German, a lawyer named Philip Camerarius, wrote the following account of two educated deaf people who used gestures, reading and writing, and speechreading to communicate:

> In our city there still live a man and a woman of respected and decent parentage who are both distinguished by a special talent. Although Nature had made both brother and sister deaf and dumb, yet they both know how to read fluently and write with a good style and draw up tradesmen's accounts. The man gathers from gestures what he must do and if no pen is available, he expresses his views by gesturing with his hand: he also excels in all forms of dice games which are popular with us and only those who are good at arithmetic can play. In needlework and fine weaving the woman easily outstrips others of her age. Amongst the astonishing talents which Nature has given them as compensation the most wonderful is that on occasion they seem to understand what is said from the movements of the lips. They frequently go to church and one might say that by watching attentively they seem to understand with their eyes as others do with their ears. When they wish, they can write out the sermon or prayers without any help and learn the feast-day texts by heart like other people. When the name of Christ is pronounced in Church, they raise their hats and genuflect before any of the others.[11]

The appearance of Alberti's and Camerarius's accounts in the late sixteenth century was not mere coincidence. A new interest in learning was leading some scholars to pay attention to deaf people and to question the nature of language, whether it could be conveyed by signs or by lip movements, or whether it required speech. These issues had been raised before, for example by Augustine and by monks who were sworn to silence but nevertheless needed to communicate and did so with signs and fingerspelling, but it reached a new urgency in the seventeenth and particularly the eighteenth century.

This was a period when literacy, the ability to read and to write, gained new importance. Printed books were becoming common. People and goods moved about in Europe, England, and America. The individual who could not read and write was increasingly at a disadvantage, especially in the rapidly growing cities. Deaf people may have fit easily and relatively comfortably into the illiterate rural life shared by most people throughout history, but in a new literate world they would be in serious difficulty—handicapped—without special education. Thus, it is not surprising that with the seventeenth century, medical and theological musings over deafness gave way to literature about the education of deaf people.

2

To Educate
a Deaf Person

Ultimately, schools brought deaf people together, forming a context within which they would develop their own cultural communities. By the nineteenth century residential institutions had become the dominant pattern in deaf education. These schools concentrated large numbers of deaf individuals, drawing them into regular contact with each other and creating shared experiences that transcended the merely physical aspects of their deafness. This process began in France and then blossomed elsewhere, particularly in the United States. The first attempts to educate deaf children, however, were not made in a group setting; rather, they were made by families that could afford to hire private tutors to provide individual instruction.

The earliest records of deaf education come from Spain. In the late sixteenth and early seventeenth centuries the Iberian nation was politically and economically stronger than it ever had been or would be again, and its intellectual advances were great. Spaniards recently had vanquished their Moslem conquerors, unified their country under Catholic monarchs, and established Spanish rule over the Western Hemisphere's wealthy Aztec and Inca empires. They drew from the Americas vast quantities of silver and gold that allowed merchants and the nobility to lead opulent, leisurely lives. Within this milieu, wealthy Spaniards who were the parents of deaf children could afford to hire learned individuals to instruct their children, and so the literature of deaf education commenced.

MELCHOR DE YEBRA

The first Spaniard to document a method for communicating with deaf people was a monk of the sixteenth century, Fray Melchor de Yebra. Familiar with a hand alphabet used by Catholic brotherhoods sworn to vows of silence, Melchor de Yebra published drawings of standardized handshapes that represented the letters of the Spanish alphabet. He reasoned that knowledge of the handshapes would be useful "for all those whose function is to assist the dying." He wrote that priests could take the confessions, by means of fingerspelling, of people who had lost the ability to speak but who were still conscious and desired to confess before dying. Melchor de Yebra claimed that he knew an instance of a man on his deathbed who could still fingerspell, although he was too ill to speak, and wished to confess by this means. The poor fellow, however, could find no one to understand his hand alphabet and thus "died with an anxious soul and desiring to make his wishes known."

A similar communication barrier might occur with repentant deaf Catholics any time, not just at the point of death, and thus Melchor de Yebra wrote that his finger alphabet also would be "of service to confessors to enable them to talk to penitents who are hard-of-hearing and to answer them when they know how to make themselves understood with hand signs." Fingerspelling could be more generally useful for religious purposes among deaf people, the monk concluded, for "it can be employed to console other deaf people who have learnt the hand alphabet because they have been obliged to do so in order to be able to converse with other people."[1]

Melchor de Yebra's discussion of fingerspelling is instructive for two reasons. First, he implied that communication by means of a hand alphabet was not unusual, or at least not unknown, in sixteenth-century Spain. He wrote of deaf people "who have learnt the hand alphabet" already. The hand alphabet presumably originated among Catholic brotherhoods and then was incorporated into the communication pattern of some deaf individuals. Exactly how this transmission from the brotherhoods to deaf people occurred is not clear from the historical record, but it may have happened when deaf boys were sent into monasteries to be educated or when monks were brought into the homes of wealthy families to teach their deaf children. In any case, it indicates that fingerspelling originated for a particular religious purpose and then was adapted for a primarily secular function. The second important point is that the hand alphabet Melchor de Yebra published is nearly identical to that used by deaf Americans in the twentieth century, and must be considered the source of the hand-shapes now used in the United States and France. It will be familiar to all who know American Sign Language. None of the original writing of Fray Melchor de Yebra has survived, but his work is known through the efforts of another Spaniard, Juan Pablo Bonet.

JUAN PABLO BONET

Juan Pablo Bonet, who worked for a wealthy Spanish family with deaf children, reproduced Melchor de Yebra's fingerspelling chart in a 1620 book. Titled *Simplification of the Letters of the Alphabet and Method of Teaching Deaf-Mutes to Speak*, this is the earliest volume about deaf education known to exist.[2] Pablo Bonet did not discuss sign language in this text, for his object was to teach oral language, but he did mention the use of his predecessor's hand alphabet. Pablo Bonet viewed fingerspelling as a means of teaching a deaf child to speak, read, and write Spanish. The purpose of his volume was to demonstrate a methodology for teaching a deaf child language so that he (only male children were educated) could be successfully integrated with hearing society. This object could be achieved only if the deaf child was forced to interact in a useful way with the hearing people around him. Thus Pablo Bonet wrote, "in a house where there is a deaf-mute, all who can read should be acquainted with this [hand] alphabet, in order to converse with him," but the deaf person "should reply by word of mouth to the questions put to him, even though he may err in pronunciation of his replies."[3]

In a remarkable passage that very nearly describes exactly the pedagogical method Alexander Graham Bell would attempt 250 years later with his deaf pupil, George Sanders, Pablo Bonet elaborated on the importance of forcing the deaf child to use spoken language to describe that with which he was most familiar, his own personal experiences. "In order that the deaf-mute may become intelligent and capable," he wrote, "it will be an important part of his education that he be asked every evening what he has done in the daytime; and though, which will certainly be the case, he does not at first answer

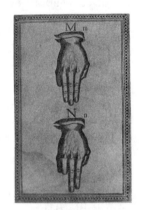

The Fingerspelling Chart of Fray Melchor de Yebra.

correctly, he must be asked again and again." Pablo Bonet continued, reasoning that

> as he [the deaf child] knows the names of objects and of actions he will necessarily reason that when he is asked, it is for the purpose of obliging him to say and tell us; and for this reason he must be asked all the questions used in our language, as, "What are you doing?" when he is doing anything; and if he does not know what to answer the master must reply for him, saying, "I am reading, writing, playing," etc. And similarly when he is doing nothing, that he may understand that he is not always obliged to say that he is doing something.[4]

Pablo Bonet would not be satisfied if the deaf child only learned to converse about everyday subjects, however, for he anticipated producing a broadly educated individual, one who could read and write. To achieve this goal, he urged the teacher to go slowly: "When the deaf-mute has learnt what we have taught already he must begin to read in books which are not on difficult subjects, but about easy and common things, and he must be asked to give an account of what he reads; and if he cannot, the teacher must explain to him."[5] Yet the teacher must be ever vigilant and flexible, Pablo Bonet asserted, and when the student "has made some progress in his reading, and in answering questions put to him either on the fingers or in writing, the books and the conversation may be changed at the discretion of the teacher, who will be able to judge of the pupil's capacity."[6]

Pablo Bonet believed that deaf people could learn to read, write, speak, and generally behave like hearing persons, but he did not believe that a tutor could teach a deaf child speechreading. He was most emphatic about this, and he was—in this and many other things—remarkably perceptive. "For the deaf to understand what is said to them by the motions of the lips," he asserted, "there is no teaching necessary; indeed, to attempt to teach it would be an imperfect thing" because of the differences in the way various individuals pronounce the same sound. Moreover, for a deaf person to see all the tongue, mouth, and facial movements that combine to create particular sounds, "all who speak to the deaf" would have to do so "with the mouth widely opened." This would not be a good practice, though, because the deaf person, imitating those speaking to him, would "fall into the habit of speaking with grimaces, seeking to utter what he has to say with the same mouthing that is used in speaking to him, which would be a great fault." Some deaf people, Pablo Bonet concluded, could read speech, but this skill was due only to "great attention on their part . . . and not to the skill of the master."[7] Even then, when deaf people

> attain to this power it is not with sufficient certainty to sustain an argument or a conversation, but only for common-place phrases, which are of such frequent use that the deaf-mute catches the meaning even without seeing the movements of their formation; his reason here also coming into play and aiding him to mark the action of the speaker, the person and the subject of which he is conversing, and the time and occasion of the theme.[8]

Pablo Bonet's final comment about deaf people was both accurate and humane, and it was far in advance of his time. *Simplification of the Letters of the Alphabet*, he wrote, showed "that deaf mutes are not really so, as far as speaking and reasoning are concerned, but are simply deaf, and capable of learning any language or science."[9] With widespread acceptance of this idea, formal education for deaf people could not be far behind.

SPAIN'S IMPACT

By the middle of the seventeenth century reports of Spain's success in educating a few deaf offspring of noble families spread elsewhere in Europe. One of the people who disseminated information about the then-curious phenomenon of educated, speaking deaf people was Sir Kenelm Digby. An Englishman, Digby visited Spain in 1623 with the Prince of Wales, the heir to the English throne. While in Madrid, Spain's capital, Digby met a deaf nobleman, Don Luis de Velasco. Don Luis's skills apparently overwhelmed Digby, and the naive traveler reported accomplishments so remarkable that all oral teachers since must surely have been envious.

Don Luis, Digby wrote, "was borne Deafe, so Deafe, that if a Gun were shot off close by his eare he could not heare it." Nevertheless, a priest taught him to speak "as distinctly as any man whoever." But this was not all. In addition to speaking flawlessly, Don Luis also understood from speechreading "so perfectly what others said, that he would not lose a word in a whole dayes conversation."[10] Digby reported that Don Luis could even recognize an accent by watching a person speak and reproduce that accent exactly with his own voice. Don Luis, Digby concluded, could perform not only these remarkable feats, he also could lipread whispers and follow conversations word for word although separated from a speaker by "the distance of a large chamber's breadth."[11]

Digby's claims stretch the modern observer's credulity, but the fact remains that seventeenth-century Europeans were beginning to look closely at deaf people and the communication process.

THE POWER OF SIGNS

The new interest in communication was evident in Anthony Deusing's *The Deaf and Dumb Man's Discourse*. Originally published in 1656 in Groningen, Holland—and then translated into English and published by George Sibscota in England in 1670—Deusing's book displayed sophisticated intuitive understanding, demonstrating that respect for signs and understanding of the communication processes of deaf persons were possible, perhaps even common, more than three hundred years ago. Signs, he wrote, may be considered like reading and writing, "by which the Conceptions of the mind are laid open to the sight, as well as they are by speech to the Ear." Deusing believed that "Mutes themselves" use signs "in lieu of speech" to "conceive the Sentiments of other mens minds." Deusing perceived no limits to the ability of signs to convey thought. Reasoning from his own experience with "obvious examples among us," by which he probably meant deaf people well known to his readers, Deusing said that people who were "originally" deaf used "gestures and various motions of the body" to "readily and clearly declare their mind to those with whom they have been often conversant."[12]

Deusing's ability to perceive accurately the communication situation of deaf people is apparent from his remarks about signs and their use. The deaf persons who use signs in place of speech, he noted, are those "originally Dumb, and Deaf," that is, those who were born deaf or became so before they could speak and thus were presumed to be deaf from the beginning of their lives. Deusing remarks that these individuals use gestures, a commonplace observation, but he adds that gestures are supplemented by "various motions of the body."[13] Modern research into American Sign Language confirms this: sign language is not limited to motions of the hands and arms—gestures—but requires movements of other parts of the body as well to be effective.[14]

Deusing was accurate again when he qualified his remarks about the complete intelligibility of signs used by deaf people. They are effective to give and receive thoughts, he wrote, but only among persons with whom deaf people "have been often conversant."[15] In short, sign language, like any other language, is an effective communication method only in a group context when the symbolic meaning of gestures is agreed upon.

Deusing reinforced this point later when he discussed the iconicity of signs. He reasoned that particular signs, what he called the "significations of things," were not any more natural than speech. He suggested that although most signs do "shadow" some "outward" characteristic of the things they symbolize, sign languages must be learned by "Study and exercise." He concluded his discussion of this subject somewhat ambivalently, but reasonably, by writing that sign languages were neither exactly like spoken languages, which "vary among several Nations," nor were they "absolutely different."[16]

Deusing's cautious and perceptive approach to deaf communication is apparent in his treatment of speechreading, too. He wrote that deaf people "conceive many things by the gestures, motion of the Lips, and such like things" of hearing people and "sometimes understand a great part of their conceptions by such outward things." To illustrate this, Deusing remarked on a man in Groningen who was born deaf but who attended public sermons and contemplated the "Words of the Preacher with his eyes fixt upon him." Still, Deusing commented that he would have liked to have had this man "examined as to his knowledge" of the preacher's sermon. This could be readily accomplished, Deusing wrote, by the man's "Wife, or Servant, his Interpreters, whom he alwayes hath with him, and who discourse with him very nimbly by signs, of any thing whatsoever."[17]

This last comment reveals a great deal. It shows that there was a deaf man with whom Deusing was acquainted who used signs regularly. More remarkably, the passage demonstrates that this deaf individual was neither poor nor isolated: he had a hearing wife and a servant; he attended church services; and he could afford to take his wife or servant with him wherever he went to serve as his "interpreters." Deusing thus provides evidence that by the middle of the seventeenth century the idea of deaf people's using interpreters to interact with hearing people was known, perhaps even considered unremarkable, for Deusing did not try to defend his statements about this individual in Groningen. Apparently, Deusing assumed that the idea of a well-to-do deaf person's using his servant and his wife to interpret for him would be readily accepted as within the range of his readers' normal experience.

Republished in England by George Sibscota, Deusing's *Deaf and Dumb Man's Discourse* and Digby's account of deaf people in Spain, which was included in John Bulwer's *Philocophus, or, the deafe and dumbe mans friend* (1648) and in Digby's own work in 1669, contributed to a growing European literature on the subject of deafness and an assumption that deaf people could be educated. This idea reached fruition by the late eighteenth century, when private profit-making schools for deaf children existed in several western European countries, and France, through the efforts of the Abbé Charles Michel de l'Épée, pioneered free education for the deaf children of poor parents. In the United States, however, things were different.

JOHN HARROWER AND JOHN EDGE

Until well after 1800 there was no school for deaf children in the Americas, thus parents were forced to find other means to educate their deaf offspring. In the 1770s, for example, Thomas Bolling and his wife, Elizabeth Gay, sent all three of their deaf children to the Braidwood Academy, a private oral school in Scotland.[18] Francis Green, a wealthy Bostonian and father of a deaf son, in 1780 followed the Bollings' example, by enrolling his son in the Braidwood Academy.[19] This was not, however, a practical solution for educating large numbers of deaf children, for schooling in Europe was both expensive and inconvenient. The historical record—by its lack of information—indicates that most American parents of deaf children did not try to provide them with any formal education, but Samuel Edge did.

Samuel Edge was not prominent or wealthy, and the records of his attempt to educate his deaf son, John, are only sketchy. They do, however, provide the first known instance of formal instruction of a deaf child in the American colonies. They also point out the haphazard nature of education in eighteenth-century America, at least in the rural South, for the person hired to teach John Edge had no evident qualifications whatsoever.

Edge's teacher was John Harrower, a Scottish merchant from the island of Shetland. Harrower left his home in search of work in December of 1773 and made his way to London. There he had no luck finding employment.[20] Cold, hungry, without shelter, friends, or prospects, in late January he made a decision that he dutifully recorded in his diary. On Wednesday, January 26, 1774, he wrote: "I was obliged to engage to go to Virginia for four years as a schoolmaster for Bedd, Board, washing and five pound[s] during the whole time."[21] In other words, Harrower became an indentured servant, a person who agreed to provide his services for a term of four years in exchange for transportation from London to the Americas, where his labor contract would be sold to the highest bidder by the ship's captain.

On the Rappahannock River near Fredericksburg, Virginia, in May of 1774 a Colonel Daingerfield purchased Harrower's contract, called an indenture, and installed the Scot as a teacher at Belvidera, Daingerfield's plantation.[22] Although Harrower was primarily responsible for teaching Daingerfield's children, the planter allowed him to teach other children from the area as a means of earning income to supplement the meager pay he received from Daingerfield. One of these children was John Edge, as recorded in Harrower's diary:

> Tuesday, 21st. This day, Mr. Samuel Edge [a] Planter came to me and begged me to take a son of his to school who was both deaf and dum, and I consented to try what I could do with him.
>
> Thursday, 23rd. This day ent[e]red to school John Edge son to the above named Mr. Sam. Edge. [H]e is a lad about 14 years of age and is both deaf and dum.[23]

The only surviving information about the means that Harrower used to try to educate John Edge lies in the following quotation from a December, 1774, letter that Harrower wrote to his wife, who still lived in Scotland:

> I have as yet only ten scollars [students] One of which is both Deaff and Dumb and his Father pays me ten shilling[s] per Quarter for him[.] [H]e has now five Mos. [months] with [me] and I have brought him tolerably well and understand it so far, that he can write mostly for anything he wants and understand the value of every figure and can work single addition a little. [H]e is about fourteen years of age.[24]

From the account contained in this letter, it appears that Harrower made some progress with John Edge, apparently communicating with him by means of writing. Later diary entries indicate he did not have Edge as a pupil for long, only six months. For teaching the deaf lad, Harrower charged Edge's father 10 shillings per three-month quarter, twice the rate he charged parents for teaching their hearing children. Ultimately, though, Harrower earned nothing for his effort. Edge's father, first referred to by Harrower as a planter—that is, an owner of a plantation—was later termed an overseer, or manager, of another's plantation, and perhaps because of this change in fortune never paid Harrower anything at all. What eventually became of John Edge is unknown.[25]

3

Braidwood
and the Bollings

The first Americans known to have organized a school specifically for the purpose of educating deaf people were the Bollings of Virginia. Though their school did not succeed, their efforts were impressive and nearly commenced an oral—rather than signing—tradition in American schools; and they almost accomplished this in Virginia rather than in New England, the area usually considered the cradle of American education and reform. The Bollings were interested in deaf education because of the persistence of congenital deafness in the family.

BOLLINGS: THE FIRST DEAF GENERATION

The first Bolling to arrive in America, Robert, came in the middle of the seventeenth century, and he soon acquired much land and wealth in colonial Virginia.[1] The initial recorded instance of deafness among the descendants of Robert Bolling occurred in the eighteenth century, following the marriage of Thomas Bolling and his first cousin, Elizabeth Gay.[2] Cousin marriage was a common practice during colonial times, especially among wealthy planters who wished to keep the family's property intact, to be shared only among members of the clan. As a result of a common genetic trait for deafness, Thomas Bolling and Elizabeth Gay Bolling bore three children who were deaf: John (1761–1783), Mary (1765–1826), and Thomas, Jr. (1766–1836). None of the deaf children married; all three were educated.

They received their schooling at the Braidwood Academy in Edinburgh, Scotland, the eighteenth century's most famous English-

21

language school for deaf children. John Bolling went first, in 1771 when he was ten years old, and two of his letters home to his mother survive. The first, dated November 26, 1771, reflected the values of the Braidwood Academy. "I am very well and very happy," John wrote to his mother, "because I can speak and read." The second, written four years later, expressed John's hope that his deaf brother and sister would soon join him: "I will be very kind to them and do them all the service I can. I have been long expecting to see them," he concluded, "and shall be glad how soon they come." John also showed his desire to return to Virginia: "I often think with pleasure of the happiness I shall enjoy with you all when I come home."[3] Assuming that the letters reflected John's writing, not that of his teacher at Braidwood's school, they demonstrate that he had, indeed, learned to write in fairly correct English.

Perhaps because of the Braidwoods' success with John, in 1775 his parents decided to send Polly (as Mary was called) and Thomas, Jr., to Scotland as well, where they stayed longer than they might have under different historical circumstances. The American Revolution, beginning in 1776 and continuing until 1783, made sea travel unsafe between England and her rebellious colonies; thus, all three deaf Bolling children remained at the Braidwood Academy until 1783. Their return home was accompanied by tragedy, however, as described in Thomas Bolling's letter of October 1783 to Thomas Braidwood. "My children," he wrote,

John Bolling was the oldest of Thomas and Elizabeth Bolling's three deaf children. He attended the Braidwood Academy in Scotland from 1771 to 1783 and died shortly after his return to the United States.

all arrived at Hampton [Virginia], very well, on 7th July, after a ten weeks passage, where I met them, and got home with them, on the 14th since which, [we] have experienced a great deal of horror. They were all taken sick soon after getting home, and [we] have had the misfortune to loose [sic] my poor Dear Son Jon[.] [H]e was taken with a Billious Fever on 29th Agst. and struggled with his disorder with as much patience as ever a poor soul did, 'till the 11th October at which time he expired.[4]

The death of the Bollings' oldest deaf son only three months after he arrived home from a twelve-year separation from his parents and family must have been a great shock to the Bollings.

John's long education in Scotland was an expense the Bollings could have done without. Thomas Bolling's letter to Thomas Braidwood, in which he recounted the death of John, included a discussion of the Bollings' financial problems; they had been unable or unwilling to pay the Braidwoods the expensive tuition of their children. "As to the Bill due you, for the education of my children," Bolling wrote, "you may assure yourself it shall be paid." It had not been paid sooner, Bolling explained, because of damage caused by the revolutionary war, specifically by the actions of England's Lord Cornwallis, who had indeed destroyed much along his march through Virginia. As Bolling explained, Cornwallis's army "burnt a very large tobacco house for me, with all the tobacco I had made for two years, a good deal of corn, and destroyed many other things too tedious to trouble

Thomas Bolling, a descendant of Pocohantas and John Rolfe, had three deaf children in the eighteenth century and sent them all to Scotland to be educated at the Braidwood Academy.

you with."[5] The Bollings' inability or unwillingness to pay the Braid-woods continued into the nineteenth century, by which time another generation of deaf Bollings also needed education.

BOLLINGS: THE SECOND DEAF GENERATION

The deaf children in the next generation were William Albert, born in 1797, and Mary, born in 1808. Both were the offspring of William Bolling—a hearing son of Thomas Bolling—and his first cousin, Mary Randolph. Unlike his father, William Bolling did not want to send his deaf children abroad to be educated. The reasons for his reluctance to do so are unclear. In a letter he stated that he was afraid to send William Albert abroad without a companion, "some friend with whom he had been in the habit of associating"; moreover, he said that the boy possessed a "meek and affectionate disposition" that deterred the father from separating from him.[6] Although this may have been true, other reasons probably included the still unpaid debt to the Braidwood Academy, dwindling Bolling financial resources, and the desire of Americans to establish themselves as independent of England in all respects, including their children's education. Whatever the Bolling family's motivations, by 1812 they still had not resolved the problem of finding suitable educational opportunities for their deaf son and presumably their daughter, though they do not mention her. Thus they were pleased to learn in 1812 that someone had come to America to establish a school for deaf children.

The newcomer was none other than John Braidwood, the grand-son of the founder of the Braidwood Academy, who arrived in the United States in February of 1812 and immediately advertised his intention to form a school for deaf students. Braidwood appeared to be qualified: not only did he have the most famous name in deaf education outside of continental Europe, but he also had headed the family school in England from 1810 to 1812. Ambitious but plagued by personal problems, he decided to leave England and emigrate to the United States, where he planned to make his fortune, as his family before him had made their fortune in the British Isles, by selling his expertise in deaf education.

Soon after his arrival on this side of the Atlantic, Braidwood was approached by two fathers of deaf children, Dr. Mason Fitch Cogswell of Connecticut and William Bolling of Virginia. Cogswell, a prominent physician, had one deaf daughter, Alice, and he was anxious to open in New England a school for her and for other deaf youngsters. Toward this purpose he and a Connecticut attorney who had five deaf children already had applied to the state government for subsidy until their institution could become self-supporting, but they needed to employ someone familiar with deaf education to work with them.[7] Thus Cogswell, upon reading of Braidwood's arrival in the United States, wrote to him and proposed a meeting to discuss the possibility of the Scot's becoming the school's instructor.[8] Desiring to establish his own school, Braidwood apparently declined Cogswell's offer, for there is no evidence of further correspondence between them. If Braidwood had accepted Cogswell's proposition, it is likely that American deaf education would have developed differently than it ultimately did.

Braidwood also initially rejected Bolling's offer to meet with him. Bolling wrote to Braidwood on March 17, 1812, inviting him to travel to the Bolling plantation "for the purpose of communicating with each other more fully than can be done by letter, on an affair which is to me of so much importance." In particular, Bolling suggested that Braidwood temporarily live with the Bollings and tutor William Albert "previous to the necessary arrangements you will have to make for a permanent establishment [of a school for deaf children], towards the accomplishment of which the deep interest I feel on the subject will ensure to you every aid in my power."[9] This generous offer, however, was spurned by the ambitious Braidwood, who was not interested in becoming a schoolmaster in rural Virginia.

BRAIDWOOD'S SCHEMES

Braidwood had in mind opening a school in Philadelphia, the largest and most cosmopolitan city in the United States in 1812. There, he hoped to realize his dream of founding a "seminary similar to our Institution in England," as he wrote to Bolling. Philadelphia had the advantage, over either New England or Virginia, of being a central location, perfect for drawing students from the North and the South. Braidwood did promise to spend a few days with Bolling at some time in the future, and he closed his letter by expressing the hope that Bolling would be comfortable sending his deaf son to Braidwood's school when it opened.[10] But the school never did open.

By May of 1812 Braidwood had changed his plans and determined to found his school in Baltimore, Maryland, rather than Philadelphia. He then advertised to attract students to his "Institution for the Deaf and Dumb, and for Removing Impediments in Speech." In an advertisement in a Richmond, Virginia, newspaper, Braidwood explained that his institution was "calculated to restore to society an unfortunate class of our fellow-creatures, who from being deprived of the Education they are so capable of receiving are excluded from the knowledge of every thing except the immediate objects of sense." Braidwood claimed he would "restore" the "unfortunate class" by teaching the students "to speak and read distinctly, to write and understand accurately the principles of Language." This was not all. Pupils also would learn "Arithmetic, Geography" and "every part of Education & Science." Indeed, the deaf students would understand "every branch of Education that may be necessary to qualify them for any situation in life."[11] Braidwood's plans were grandiose, and they were totally beyond his capacity.

By the fall of 1812 he still had not established a school anywhere. Instead, he was in a New York City jail for debt, probably caused by his drinking and gambling, afflictions that plagued him until he died. While in jail, he temporarily abandoned his plan to operate his own institution for deaf children and asked Bolling for assistance, which the father—now more than ever anxious to procure education for his son—granted.

COBBS SCHOOL

From late 1812, after he was bailed out of prison, until 1815 Braidwood lived with the Bolling family on their Virginia plantation, named Cobbs, and tutored their deaf children. He had not given up completely on his ambitions, however, and in March of 1815, he finally opened a school in the Bolling family mansion.[12] There he had at least five students: William Albert Bolling, George Lee Turberville, John Hancock, John M. Scott, and Marcus Flournoy.[13] William Albert's deaf uncle, Thomas Bolling, Jr., also was in residence at Cobbs during most of the year and a half that the school functioned.

Although the school was short-lived, it could have gained a more permanent foothold if the third president of the United States, Thomas Jefferson, had been sympathetic to deaf education. Apparently, he was not, even though his sister, Martha Jefferson, had married John Bolling, the uncle of the first three deaf Bollings.[14] In January of 1816 Jefferson was approached about the possibility of moving

Braidwood's school from Cobbs to Charlottesville, Virginia, and associating it with the University of Virginia. Jefferson—the person who wrote that "all men are created equal"—responded negatively:

> I should not like to have [Braidwood's school] made a member of our college. The objects of the two institutions are fundamentally different. The one is science; the other, mere charity. It would be gratuitously taking a boat in tow, which may impede, but cannot aid the motion of the principal institution.[15]

Instead of becoming part of the University of Virginia, the Cobbs school closed in the fall of 1816 when the pitiful Braidwood, true to his former habits, disappeared from Cobbs and thus ended the first school for deaf children in the United States.

Braidwood did not disappear completely from the annals of American deaf education, however, for Bolling again rescued him from destitution and brought him back to Virginia in 1817. This time, the now-wary Bolling took Braidwood to a minister named John Kirkpatrick who operated a school in Manchester, near Richmond, Virginia. The agreement among Braidwood, Bolling, and Kirkpatrick stipulated that Braidwood would, in association with Kirkpatrick, establish a school for deaf children in Manchester and also would teach Kirkpatrick the methods necessary to instruct deaf pupils.[16] By the middle of 1818, though, the Reverend Kirkpatrick was disgusted with Braidwood's habits and threw him out, ending a second futile attempt to found in Virginia a school for deaf Americans.

THE BOLLING-BRAIDWOOD FAILURE

Other than providing a rudimentary education for a few deaf children, the Braidwood-Bolling episode ultimately produced nothing of permanent consequence. It illustrates, nevertheless, what might have been. Braidwood twice came very close to founding private institutions patterned after those of his family in Edinburgh, Scotland, and London, England. Those schools, limited to serving the deaf children of wealthy families and based on a strictly oral approach to deaf education, would have been radically different from the first successful institution for deaf pupils, the American Asylum for the Deaf and Dumb (later renamed the American School for the Deaf) in Hartford, Connecticut.

The Braidwood-Bolling failure to found American deaf education illustrates, as well, the inherent difficulties of that task and the
conditions that were necessary to accomplish it. Bolling never built
the community support, the network of interested influential citizens,
that Cogswell (and later Thomas Hopkins Gallaudet and Laurent
Clerc) so carefully constructed before opening the American School.
The latter school began its life with strong financial commitments
from wealthy individuals, many of them people with deaf offspring of
their own who thus had a personal stake in the school's viability.
Quickly after the school opened Cogswell, Gallaudet, and Clerc acted
to secure political support for their fledgling enterprise. There is no
evidence that Bolling attempted anything similar.

Finally, Bolling chose the wrong man to head his school. Not
only did Braidwood suffer from personal difficulties but he was motivated by nothing more than a desire to make his fortune, to earn
enough money to support his habits. Cogswell's choice to found his
school, Thomas Hopkins Gallaudet, was a different sort of person
altogether. Unlike Jefferson, he did not believe that the task of educating deaf persons was "mere charity." Moreover, he was driven not by
greed but by deeply held religious conviction and a personal commitment to the betterment of humankind. Like his French predecessor,
Épée, Gallaudet would do whatever was necessary, at whatever personal sacrifice, to assure that the American School served the greater
glory of his God.

4

A Permanent School

The first permanent school for deaf Americans opened its doors on April 15, 1817, in Hartford, Connecticut. It was christened the Connecticut Asylum for the Education and Instruction of Deaf and Dumb Persons. Today it is known as the American School for the Deaf and is correctly viewed as the predecessor of the modern state-supported residential institutions for deaf children.[1]

There was nothing inevitable about the form that deaf education assumed in the early nineteenth century, for there were false starts before the American School achieved success. It seems clear, however, that by the 1820s some kind of school for deaf pupils would exist in the United States. The American population was growing rapidly. Schools were becoming popular, as many people believed that an educated citizenry was necessary to economic growth and a stable democratic government. Furthermore, this was an age of reforms, a time of religious revival and social ferment. It was also an age of American nationalism. The idea of sending deaf children to Europe for education, though it had been done previously, was deemed unnecessary, perhaps even unpatriotic in a young nation trying to assert itself.[2]

The American School established a pattern of deaf education that remained dominant in the United States until long after the Civil War. First, the low incidence of deafness in the general population required that the school serve a wide geographic area in order to have sufficient students to form classes, and thus it had to be residential: pupils simply could not commute daily from homes tens or even hundreds of miles from Hartford. The students lived and studied together in one place, separated from their families and to an extent isolated from hearing society. In effect, the residential schools became surrogate parents; the language and behaviors learned there became more influential to the lives of their residents than were their previous experiences in their biological families. Within the walls of the academy, older deaf children would pass on to each new generation of deaf children the cultural attributes that marked deaf Americans as a distinct subculture within America.

A second significant aspect of the American School was its funding. Although Cogswell failed to receive government support for his school before it opened, soon after its establishment the American School did get financial assistance from the state of Connecticut and from the federal government.[3] This freed the American School, and its descendants, from the vagaries of charitable contributions and from charging high tuition.

The third and fourth important features of the American School were interrelated: the usual communication method in the school, from its inception, was sign language, not speech and speechreading; and deaf teachers were prominent.[4] Indeed, the person initially hired to teach all the other instructors at the American School was himself deaf, and the school actively recruited its best students to become instructors after they graduated.

SOLID FOUNDATIONS

Three men share the responsibility for founding the American School and assuring that it did not collapse the way its Virginia predecessors did. They were Cogswell, a frustrated but tenacious and perceptive parent whose daughter Alice had become deaf from meningitis at age two; Gallaudet, a superb orator and zealous minister; and Laurent Clerc, a brilliant and ambitious young deaf teacher at the Royal Institution for the Deaf and Dumb in Paris.[5] These three individuals came together almost accidentally.

Unlike his southern counterpart, William Bolling, Cogswell early realized the importance of developing a network of political and financial support to open a school for educating his deaf child. Himself a prominent New Englander, Cogswell used his influence and that of other well-connected parents of deaf children to convince ministers in Connecticut to conduct a census of their communities to ascertain the number of deaf children in the state. Undertaken between 1812

Mason Fitch Cogswell, a Yale graduate and Hartford, Connecticut physician, organized the American School for the Deaf so that his deaf daughter Alice could receive an education in the United States.

MASON F. COGSWELL, M.D.

and 1815, the census determined that Connecticut had eighty-four deaf people, surely enough to warrant an educational establishment.[6] Census taking also put Cogswell in touch with other deaf parents, and he exploited the information he could gather from them.

One of the parents with whom Cogswell worked to lay the foundations of American deaf education was a lawyer named Sylvester Gilbert. Gilbert had five deaf children, and Cogswell believed that he could assist in publicizing the need for a school and in convincing the Connecticut state legislature to grant money for the school's support. In 1812 Gilbert agreed to work with Cogswell toward this objective. He recommended putting notices in all the newspapers in the state "for the purpose of exciting some attention to" their plan of organizing a school for deaf children. The notices, Gilbert continued, would serve "*as an entering wedge*" in their project.[7] Five years later Gilbert's deaf daughter, Mary, was one of the original twenty-one students at the American School.[8]

Gilbert was involved with Cogswell from early on and supported the school project in a number of ways, but Cogswell also enlisted financial commitments from as many well-to-do parents of deaf children as he could. Among these parents was Eliphalet Kimball of Salem, Massachusetts.

Kimball, like Cogswell and Gilbert, had a deaf daughter. Reasoning that Kimball might therefore have a natural sympathy with the idea of education for deaf children, Cogswell requested that Gallaudet approach him to ascertain his interest in supporting deaf education. Gallaudet wrote to Kimball in 1813, specifically requesting a cash donation to assist in sending someone to Europe to learn about methods for educating deaf children prior to establishing a school in Hartford. Kimball replied shrewdly. In an 1814 letter to Cosgwell he wrote that Gallaudet's plan "appears to me and to some of my friends with whom I have conversed and whose opinion I value, to be judicious." However, he continued:

> I should like to be informed whether those who contribute towards the expense of a person's going to Europe are to be favoured in any way hereafter, or whether the money advanced is considered merely a donation towards the establishment of an institution to which they may have access in common with others?
>
> I should probably be influenced [Kimball concluded] as to the amount I might furnish (which would be from one to two hundred dollars as I could not conveniently share more at present) by the answer to this inquiry which I would thank you to give me and I will then specify the sum—[9]

Cogswell certainly was not averse to this kind of dealing, realizing perhaps that it held out the best promise of successfully raising money through somewhat self-interested philanthropy. Any person who donated $100 or more to the American School's founding was made a director of the institution. Among the first directors was Eliphalet Kimball.

Gilbert, Kimball, and other wealthy New Englanders were important to Cogswell's project: they contributed money, gave their considerable political support, and helped to sustain Cogswell through the long years of planning and scheming required to construct an institutional environment within which to educate his favorite daughter. In terms of the ultimate shape that environment would take, however, the most important hearing individual was Gallaudet.

THOMAS HOPKINS GALLAUDET

The eldest of twelve children, Thomas Hopkins Gallaudet was a fervently religious evangelical Christian whose life was shaped by his moral commitments and by his nearly constant ill health. He began his adulthood as a spectacularly successful student: he graduated first in his class from Yale University at age seventeen in 1805. Two years

A sickly congregational minister, Thomas Hopkins Gallaudet, was one of the three men most responsible for establishing the American School for the Deaf—the first permanent school for deaf Americans.

later he received a master of arts from Yale, and in 1812 he entered Andover Theological Seminary, from which he was graduated in 1814 and ordained as a Congregational minister. Illness, however, prevented him from holding a full-time pastorship, and he lived at his family's home in Hartford, Connecticut, where—fortuitously—his neighbor was the eminent surgeon Cogswell.[10]

Cogswell's daughter, Alice, interested Gallaudet, perhaps arousing his Christian sympathy, and he tried to teach her to read. In this he had some success, teaching her to spell "hat" and a few other words. He also began working with Cogswell to gather support for and interest in an American school for deaf children. By 1815 he and Cogswell had raised enough money to send someone to Europe to learn there the techniques used to educate deaf persons, for Gallaudet felt frustrated and inadequate in his feeble attempts to break through Alice's deafness. At Cogswell's urging, Gallaudet agreed to undertake this journey himself, despite his ill health and intense self-doubt about his ability. Thus in the summer of 1815 he embarked for England.[11]

Gallaudet's original plan focused on the British Isles. He hoped to study there for a short time at a school for deaf children and then return to Connecticut with his new-found knowledge. In England, however, Gallaudet encountered frustration and the rigidities of a system dominated by the Braidwoods and committed to the proposition that the teaching of deaf people should be a money-making, private-school, enterprise. Eventually the Braidwoods agreed to take on Gallaudet as an apprentice at their school in England, but only if he promised to stay with them for several years and to keep their techniques secret, not to share them with others. These terms were unacceptable to Gallaudet.[12] The American reformer was motivated primarily by benevolence, and he abhorred secrecy and profit making at the expense of downtrodden people; therefore, he had no interest in this scheme. Furthermore, he had no desire to remain in England for several years. While in London, however, he discovered a way around the roadblocks established by the Braidwood family.

In July of 1815 the Abbé Sicard, successor to Épée as head of the Royal Institution for the Deaf in Paris, was in London with two highly accomplished former students of the Royal Institution, Jean Massieu and Laurent Clerc, and a young deaf boy named Armand Goddard.[13] Gallaudet saw his chance. Knowing of Sicard and the Paris institution through a publication of Sicard's that Cogswell had obtained and given to him, Gallaudet introduced himself to the Parisian and, he wrote to Cogswell, "was very cordially received."[14] Sicard gave to Gallaudet a free ticket to one of the exhibitions Sicard and his students were holding in London. In these "lectures," as Gallaudet termed them, Sicard would discuss his theories of deaf education and then invite the audience to ask questions of Massieu and Clerc in order to determine for themselves the success of French educational methods. The intelligence and wit of the answers delivered—on chalk-

Roch Ambroise Sicard succeeded the Abbé de l'Épée as head of the Royal Institution for the Deaf in Paris. In 1815 he met Thomas Hopkins Gallaudet and invited him to study at the Royal Institution.

Jean Massieu, graduate of the Royal Institution in Paris and a teacher there, met Thomas Hopkins Gallaudet in London in 1815. His knowledge and accomplishments helped convince Gallaudet of the benefits of the French system of education for deaf persons.

JⁿMASSIEU.

boards—by Massieu and Clerc overwhelmed Gallaudet. Clerc, for example, gave the following response to the question "What is education?": "Education is the care," Clerc wrote on his slate, "which is taken to cultivate the minds of youth, to elevate their hearts & to give them the knowledge of the science, & of art that is necessary to teach them to conduct well in the world." In sum, Gallaudet reported to Cogswell, Massieu and Clerc "answered with wonderful dispatch & propriety." Here, then, was a model of what education could do for deaf children, and it was made accessible to Gallaudet by Sicard's generous invitation to visit the Royal Institution in Paris, where he would be received with "every attention and facility."[15]

And he was. After failing to receive the support he wished from the Braidwoods, in 1816 Gallaudet went to Paris and began studying at the Royal Institution, which he described in simple language in a letter to Alice:

> The school for the Deaf and Dumb here is a very large building of stone. In front of it is a large yard, and behind it a fine garden. There are nearly 90 scholars, boys and girls. I have seen the lowest class several times. There are fifteen boys in it. The master is a Romish [that is, Roman Catholic] Clergyman. . . . In the room are a number of large black boards, on which the scholars write with chalk. I wrote on these boards and talked with the boys. They understood me very well. One told me he was from the same country as I. But was mistaken. He was

The Royal Institution for the Deaf in Paris. Laurent Clerc was educated here, and Thomas Hopkins Gallaudet studied French teaching methods here in the spring of 1816.

from Guadeuloupe, [*sic*] an island in the West Indies. Another said he was from the United States, from Georgia.

This last individual may have been Marcus Flournoy, who also attended the Cobbs school in Virginia and was from a wealthy Georgia slaveholding family that easily could have sent him to Paris to be educated. In any case, Gallaudet's letter to Alice also revealed that he was rapidly becoming homesick, and his intensely Protestant conscience was upset by the ways of a Catholic city. He concluded his letter with these provincial (and prejudiced) observations:

> I had rather live in Hartford than Paris. You would be very sorry to see the Sabbath kept so badly in Paris. Most of the shops are open, and people buy and sell goods. And the Theatres are open and but few people go to church, particularly in the afternoon. How much we ought to be sorry for such a people, and to thank God that it is not so in Connecticut.[16]

In the spring of 1816 Gallaudet faced a crisis. He was homesick— tired of living away from New England and among the Catholics of

Paris—and he was running out of money. By chance he met an American friend, captain of the *Mary Augusta,* a ship that would soon sail
for the United States, who suggested that Gallaudet return home with
him. Another friend who had been living in Paris also encouraged
Gallaudet to return, for he, too, planned to embark on the *Mary
Augusta.* Gallaudet longed to join his comrades, but he doubted
whether he was, as he wrote to Sicard, "sufficiently qualified for my
intended employment, the instruction of the deaf and dumb." He
could not go home without satisfying his duty to the people who had
raised money for his journey; to do so would have been to commit a
wrong to them and would have terminated what Gallaudet had come
to believe was his mission. Laurent Clerc, however, supplied Gallaudet with a way out of this dilemma, and in the course of doing so
forever altered the history of deaf Americans.[17]

LAURENT CLERC

Clerc was, in May of 1816, a thirty-year-old teacher at the Royal Institution for the Deaf in Paris. He had arrived there eighteen years before
as a student and had proven himself brilliant. Along with his former
teacher, Massieu, Clerc was one of the successfully educated deaf men
whom Sicard used in his exhibitions (an idea later successfully copied
by American institutions) to garner support for the efforts of the
Royal Institution.[18] Gallaudet first made Clerc's acquaintance in London and then got to know him during his stay in Paris. The exact
sequence of events that led Gallaudet and Clerc to decide to work
together is not altogether clear, but, according to Gallaudet and one
of the surviving documents written by Clerc, it was the deaf Frenchman who in May of 1816 volunteered "of his own accord" (Gallaudet's words) to go with Gallaudet to the United States.[19]

This seemed a perfect solution for Gallaudet's dilemma, and it
offered opportunities for Clerc that were not available if he remained
in France. The advantages that Gallaudet would gain seem, in retrospect, obvious: He would be able to leave Paris almost immediately,
even though he was not yet ready to assume the leadership of deaf
education in the United States. Clerc was not only skilled in teaching
deaf students, but he had the virtue of being an exemplary model
of what a deaf person could become—educated, industrious, socially
skilled. Therefore, once Gallaudet and Clerc were back in the United
States, the latter would be especially useful to Gallaudet's and Cogs-

Laurent Clerc was the deaf Frenchman who, with Thomas Hopkins Gallaudet and Mason Fitch Cogswell, founded the American School for the Deaf and established the American system of deaf education.

well's ongoing attempts to raise money for their school and to convince skeptical governments of the advantages to be accrued by providing for the education of the country's deaf people.

Yet there were risks involved for Gallaudet, too. Although Clerc was surely a skilled teacher in the institution that had been his home for virtually all his adolescent and adult life, there was no guarantee that he would be equally successful in the different, unstructured, and new environment of a school in Hartford, Connecticut. The Parisian culture he knew was radically different from that of a provincial New England city. In the United States he would be separated by a several weeks' voyage from his friends, teachers, family, and colleagues. Clerc's English also was suspect. Although he did know some English before leaving Paris, he was by no means fluent.[20] Whether he would be able to learn it well enough to communicate in writing with hearing Americans remained doubtful. And he would have to communicate by writing. Clerc did not speak. Apparently he had become deaf at age one, before his speech was developed, and he had given up speaking altogether while still a student.[21] Gallaudet could not be certain, either, that Cogswell or the committee that had been brought together to found the American School would approve the money necessary to pay Clerc's salary. This matter apparently never had been discussed when it was assumed that Gallaudet, alone, would become the head teacher in the new school. Finally, Clerc was a Catholic, from a Catholic family, educated in a Catholic school managed by a

Catholic priest, in a Catholic country. How would this rest with the devout (and bigoted) Protestants of Hartford?

Clerc was hardly unaware of these difficulties and the uncertainties inherent in his decision to become Gallaudet's partner in far-off New England. He was, nevertheless, an ambitious and confident young man, perhaps one frustrated by the limited horizons of the Royal Institution for the Deaf. Thus he proceeded boldly—by proposing to accompany Gallaudet in his uncertain venture—but cautiously.

The long and detailed contract he and Gallaudet concluded on June 13, 1816, testifies to Clerc's perceptiveness and his caution. Clerc's obligations and those of Gallaudet were carefully delineated to assure that Clerc would not be exploited. He agreed that for a period of three years he would teach for six hours each weekday and for three hours on Saturday. On Sundays and holidays he was to be "entirely at liberty," and he would have six weeks of vacation annually.[22] The subjects he would teach were enumerated as follows:

> Mr. Clerc shall endeavor to give his pupils a knowledge of grammar, language, arithmetic, the globe, geography, history; of the Old Testament as contained in the Bible, and the New Testament, including the life of Jesus Christ, the Acts of the Apostles, the Epistles of St. Paul, St. John, St. Peter, and St. Jude.[23]

In addition to teaching, Clerc would be expected to "be present and assist" in public lectures given by Gallaudet, as he had aided in the demonstrations of Sicard in London. Finally, Clerc's obligations extended to a prohibition for three years against activities that might jeopardize the success of the Hartford school; that is, Clerc was not to assist potential competitors, sell his services to "any other establishment," or give any "instruction or public lectures . . . except under the direction of Mr. Gallaudet."[24]

Gallaudet's obligations were similarly detailed. He would pay Clerc 2,500 francs per year for his services; "defray all Mr. Clerc's travelling expenses from Paris to Hartford [including] food, lodging, washing, and transportation for himself and his effects, by land and water;" in Hartford supply Clerc with an apartment near the future school; serve him meals in Gallaudet's own house; and provide for Clerc's "washing, fires, lights, and attendance." At the end of his three-year contractual obligation, Clerc was free to return to France, and if he did so, Gallaudet was required to pay him 1,500 francs for traveling expenses in addition to his salary. Gallaudet also would have to pay this sum if "circumstances beyond his [Clerc's] own control" forced Clerc to return to France before the three years were completed.[25] In short, Clerc protected himself against the eventuality of the school's failure.

Clerc wisely used the contract to protect himself against two other difficulties—that Gallaudet might not be able to raise the money necessary to meet the commitments promised in the contract and that his Catholicism would create problems when he taught. Gallaudet was not a wealthy individual. If he could not convince Cogswell and the directors of the Connecticut school to pay Clerc the agreed upon sum in the manner stipulated in the contract, Clerc might face great difficulty receiving his salary. The contract, however, contained the stipulation that two of Gallaudet's friends would guarantee that Clerc would be paid. A French banker, Jean Conrad Hottinguer, and an American merchant, Sampson Vryling Stoddard Wilder, "voluntarily declared that they each and jointly constitute themselves sureties of Mr. Gallaudet on account of his engagements to Mr. Clerc as stated" in the contract. In case Gallaudet could not pay Clerc's salary, the contract stated, Hottinguer and Wilder "pledge themselves, singly and conjointly, to pay Mr. Clerc at his new place of residence [Hartford] the promised amounts in the sums and at the times previously fixed upon."[26]

Clerc wished to guarantee his religious independence among the fiercely prejudiced Protestants of Hartford, and the contract reflected this appropriate concern. It stated that although Clerc was expected to teach the religious subjects stipulated in the contract, he would not be required "to teach anything contrary to the Roman Catholic religion which he professes, and in which faith he desires to live and die." He neither would have to teach Protestant beliefs, nor would there be an expectation that Clerc would convert (though ultimately he became an Episcopalian) to a Protestant denomination. Gallaudet, the contract went on to say, would be responsible for "all matters of religious teaching which may not be in accordance" with Clerc's Catholicism.[27]

Gallaudet saw in Clerc an answer to his urgent need to return to the United States and a solution to the intolerable ignorance of deaf American children. He concluded his contract with Clerc independently, before Cogswell had more than a brief acquaintance with the name Laurent Clerc. Four days after the contract between Gallaudet and Clerc was signed, indeed, when they were already on board the *Mary Augusta*, Gallaudet wrote to Cogswell and told him what he had done. His letter to Cogswell began, "To-morrow I expect to sail from these parts in the Mary Augusta with Captain Hall, for New York, in company with Mr. S. V. S. Wilder . . . and a Mr. Clerc whom perhaps you may have heard of or seen his name mentioned in some of the papers." Gallaudet went on, "Yes, my dear friend, Providence, has most kindly provided for my study and successful return by furnishing me with the most accomplished pupil of the Abbé Sicard and one, too, who is not less recommended by probity and sweetness of his character . . . than by his rare talents."[28]

ARRIVAL IN AMERICA

After a voyage of one and a half months, Gallaudet and Clerc arrived in New York, where a much-relieved Gallaudet rhapsodized, "how great is the goodness of God in thus again conducting me in safety across the mighty deep." The time at sea had been well spent, however, with Clerc and Gallaudet each teaching the other. Gallaudet took advantage of his confinement with Clerc to work on his sign language skills, learning the system of signs and fingerspelling that Clerc had used in the Royal Institution in Paris. For Clerc, the overwhelming task at hand was to improve his English language skills. He worked assiduously, reading constantly and doing language drills that Gallaudet corrected. Gallaudet marveled at the ability of his companion: "I have not the *least doubt* that a few more months will quite make [Clerc] perfect in the more colloquial parts of our language." Clerc's fortitude and commitment drew equal praise from Gallaudet. "He has not been sick a *single* day," he wrote, "and has been the most industrious man on board, always at his books or writing."

The frustrations that Gallaudet suffered in the British Isles were now a thing of the past. "I rejoice in my disappointments at London & Edinburgh," he wrote. "God ordered them in his infinite wisdom and goodness—To him be all the glory of the success with which our undertaking has been crowned."[29]

To prove just how likely that success would be, Gallaudet sent, with a letter of his own to Cogswell, a short note written in English by Clerc, the deaf Frenchman. It represents the earliest surviving sample of Clerc's written English and gives a foretaste of the remarkable stylist he would become in a language he never heard. It is not grammatically perfect, however, and thus seems to indicate that it was in fact written by Clerc, without Gallaudet's correcting it.

> I have just arrived at New-York with my good friend Mr. Gallaudet who has often spoken to me of Dr. Cogswell & also of the amiable & interesting Alice. I long to see both, but I hope I shall soon be happy. For the means while [sic] I beg to give you all my respectfuly [sic] compliments.[30]

The pleasure and surprise with which Cogswell must have received Clerc's brief greeting is best understood by considering Cogswell's probable expectations. Until he met Clerc, Cogswell's personal experience with deaf people, so far as the historical records indicate, was limited to his daughter, and she was far from literate in English. Having grown up in an environment without sophisticated visual communication (i.e., without sign language) she had not mastered written expression. A letter she wrote to Gallaudet in December of 1816 indicates the poverty of her English skills. The letter is comprehensible, but just barely. It begins, "My Dear Thomas," and continues,

> I am very glad, you to in N York you will and come back and my home and Hartford. I will see to you and Mr. Clerc. I want to see to you and he very much. I remember very much and to you and he, how many, says you come back my home Hartford, you tell your write me do want very much know. I hope so and one week you come back and my home here.
>
> Mr. Hudson his dog and very much bad and very much wild, dog jumps on all ladies and mens and girls and boys very afraid dog jump not on me I very much afraid. My sister Mary have yes and she says me she afraid very much. My brother Mason have dog bite Mansons hand little sore, he says to me, he afraid not.[31]

Comparing this effort, albeit of an eleven-year-old without formal training, with that of Clerc, Cogswell must have been happy with Gallaudet's decision to bring Clerc back to the United States and to model the Connecticut school on the Paris institution.

In order to do so, Gallaudet and Clerc set about in earnest raising money and public support for their proposed institution. They traveled throughout New England giving lectures. Clerc, as he had done in London, demonstrated for audiences his learning and his intelligence, while Gallaudet used his substantial rhetorical skills to convince audiences that it was their responsibility as Christians to support education for those innocent individuals deprived of the privilege of learning God's ways through hearing.[32] Problems soon developed, however, in the state of New York.

Plans to educate deaf Americans were not confined to Connecticut, or to Connecticut and Virginia, in the 1810s, for they were actively developing in New York as well.[33] In January of 1817, with the American School nearly ready to open, Gallaudet and Clerc journeyed to New York to attempt to block the establishment there of a potential rival. At first they were optimistic that their lobbying efforts were successful, but on January 14 a committee voted to establish in New York City a school for deaf children, as Clerc eloquently wrote to Cogswell.

> Ah! My worthy friend, man proposes & God disposes; the meeting of this afternoon has decided in favour of another Institution here; I had expected this; the number of the Deaf & Dumb who have been enumerated [in New York City] amounting to forty-seven, a part of whom are susceptible of instruction, has been one of the principal causes for the decision.

Clerc went on to say that a committee had been formed to write a constitution for the New York school and to "petition the Legislature of N.Y. & the corporation of the City" to request financial support.[34] In this they were successful. On April 15, 1817—the same day the Connecticut Asylum actually opened its doors—the state of New York granted a charter for the New York Institution for the Deaf and Dumb. In May of 1818 the New York school received its first deaf pupils in the city's almshouse.[35]

THE CONNECTICUT ASYLUM

By the time the New York Institution began instruction of deaf children, the "Connecticut Asylum, For the Education and Instruction of Deaf and Dumb Persons," as it was formally called, before it was renamed the American School for the Deaf, was more than one year old and well on its way to establishing an American tradition of deaf education. Cogswell, Gallaudet, Clerc, and influential Yankees had raised privately about $5,000 toward the school's support. More importantly, in May of 1816 the Connecticut state legislature granted the American School a charter of incorporation and followed that with a precedent-setting action—the state granted the asylum $5,000

from government funds, thus initiating a pattern of public support
for education of disabled Americans.[36]

Among the first recipients of this governmental largess were
some important individuals and familiar names in the history of the
American deaf community. The first student to enroll was of course
Alice Cogswell; the sixth was John Brewster, Jr. Fifty-one years old
when he enrolled and deaf from birth, Brewster had been known to
the Reverend James Cogswell, Mason Cogswell's father, and he was
the first of many accomplished deaf American painters. He remained
at the American School for three years.[37] Mary Gilbert, daughter of
the prominent attorney who had assisted Cogswell in raising money
and publicizing the need for an educational institution for deaf New
Englanders, was the twelfth student admitted. Fifteenth and seventeenth were, respectively, Sophia Fowler of Guilford, Connecticut,
and Eliza C. Boardman of Whitesborough, New York.[38] The former
married Thomas Hopkins Gallaudet, and the latter became the wife
of Laurent Clerc. Sophia Fowler Gallaudet was the mother of the
founder of Gallaudet University—Edward Miner Gallaudet. She also
served as the first matron of the Columbia Institution for the Deaf,
the school that eventually became Gallaudet University.

The American School, under the leadership of Gallaudet and
Clerc, was staunchly manual in its approach to communication with
its students. The third annual report of the school discussed the issue

*Eliza Boardman, the seventeenth pupil
admitted to the American School, became
the wife of her teacher, Laurent Clerc.*

at some length, revealing the institution's deep respect for the sign language that deaf people themselves had developed.[39] There were no patronizing statements about the superiority of English or of spoken language. To the contrary, the report said that four modes of communication were employed in the school, and the most important was "the natural language of signs." The report stated that

> The *first*, [communication method] on which all the rest are founded, and without which every attempt to teach the deaf and dumb would be utterly vain and fruitless,—is the natural language of signs, originally employed by the deaf and dumb in all their intercourse with their friends and each other, singularly adapted to their necessities, and so significant and copious in its various expressions, that it furnishes them with a medium of conversation on all common topics the very moment that they meet, although, before, [they were] entire strangers to each other, and it is even used by themselves, in a vast variety of instances, to denote the invisible operations of their minds and emotions of their hearts.[40]

The other methods of communication were a standardized sign system modeled after the methodical signs developed by Épée in Paris (and perhaps similar to today's signed English), fingerspelling by means of the shapes first published by Pablo Bonet and then brought to America by Clerc, as well as writing in English. Speech and speech-reading were not taught. Indeed, the report belittled them by arguing that speech teaching had no value, for it did not contribute to students' intellectual development; moreover, it rarely worked. Articulation, the report argued, was a "comparatively useless branch of the education of the deaf and dumb. In no case is it the source of any original knowledge to the mind of the pupil."[41] Instead of wasting time with trying to teach speech, the report emphasized, the principal and instructors at the American School labored "to convey important intellectual and religious knowledge to their [students'] minds by means of the four modes of communication" mentioned.[42]

THE RELIGIOUS FACTOR

Many factors contributed to the success of the American School in establishing a permanent and successful school for deaf Americans. The political skill and influence of Cogswell was important. Clerc's ability as an educator and his willingness to leave Paris and to devote himself to American deaf education also were crucial. Another key ingredient, however, was the religious zeal that motivated Gallaudet and the people whom he convinced to support the school with their financial resources. The link between social reform and religious belief that animated Gallaudet and other reformers in early nineteenth-century America cannot be overestimated, as shown by the record of the American School.

The school's first report emphasized the importance of providing deaf people with education in order to save them. It argued that the souls of deaf people would be "rescued from intellectual darkness," and deaf individuals would "be brought to a knowledge of the truth as it is in Jesus." This accomplished, deaf Americans would "finally be found among the redeemed of the Lord."[43]

5

The Residential School Experience

Residential schools nourished the foundations of the American deaf community. Their academic and vocational instruction produced a core of educated deaf adults who shared a common language and similar experiences. Many residential school graduates became teachers themselves and thus constituted an important group with whom deaf youngsters interacted, providing models and cultural indoctrination. By 1843, six states had followed Connecticut's example and provided for state-supported or state-operated residential schools for deaf children: New York in 1818, Pennsylvania in 1820, Kentucky in 1823, Ohio in 1827, Virginia in 1838, and Indiana in 1843. Persons trained at the American School in Connecticut were instrumental in the early success of every one of these institutions. Like the school in Hartford, each of these was staunchly manual in its approach; and as had been the case in Hartford, parents of deaf students played important roles in convincing the six state governments to support the education of deaf children.[1]

Tax-supported special educational institutions freed families from the terrible dilemmas that had confronted the Cogswells and Bollings. Now, the bewildered parents of deaf children could be assured that their offspring would receive skilled instruction, on this side of the Atlantic, and at relatively low cost. Deaf children who lived in a state with a state-supported residential school usually could attend for free; those who lived in a state without its own school could, for a fee still below that of private schools or tutors, attend the school of another state. Such was the situation confronting Jane and

Samuel Tillinghast of North Carolina when they realized that their son, Thomas, born in 1833, was deaf.

THE TILLINGHASTS

The Tillinghasts of North Carolina were not as wealthy as the Bollings of Virginia or as prominent as the Cogswells of Connecticut, but they were deeply concerned about the future of Thomas and his younger deaf brother, David, born in 1841. When Thomas's deafness was first recognized, his parents reacted as most would—they immediately sought a medical remedy. Jane Tillinghast's brother, J. H. Norwood, was entrusted with this important mission when he visited New York City, where knowledge of medicine presumably was more advanced than in rural North Carolina.

What Norwood learned from the two doctors whom he consulted in New York was not promising. They said that a hard-of-hearing individual or a person who had become deafened in childhood might be cured, but they held out little hope that Thomas's congenital deafness would be amenable to their remedies. One physician, a Dr. Webster, claimed that he had had some success with surgical procedures. One such procedure involved piercing the eardrum, whereas the other required the opening of a passageway between the mouth and the middle ear. The former operation was complete foolishness and would only have caused Thomas unnecessary pain. The latter, presumably designed to make the eustachian tube functional, almost assuredly would not have given Thomas any benefit either.[2] Fortunately, Norwood had the good sense to dismiss these suggestions and turn elsewhere for assistance with his nephew. Norwood went to the New York Institution for the Deaf and Dumb, then located at Fiftieth Street, and there consulted with the principal, Harvey P. Peet.[3]

Peet was a giant in the field of deaf education in the nineteenth century. He began his career in 1822 at the American School, where he remained until 1831; he then became principal and superintendent of the New York school. He occupied the principalship for thirty-five years and was succeeded in 1866 by his son, Isaac Lewis Peet. During the long period of the elder Peet's leadership, the New York school, which once had been a weak and poorly administered establishment, became a fine and progressive institution, one of the best in the United States. Peet encouraged his faculty to take an active role in advancing the cause of deaf education. Leading by example, he pre-

Harvey P. Peet headed the New York School for the Deaf from 1831 to 1866 and was a leader in American education of deaf children.

pared and published courses of instruction for deaf people and was ready to respond to the inquiries of anxious parents or relatives like J. H. Norwood.[4]

Peet spoke at length with Norwood and gave him three pamphlets that he had written to guide parents and teachers. Norwood believed these contained "all the information . . . which can be imparted upon the subject" of educating a deaf child. The pamphlets suggested that it was "absolutely necessary" to send deaf children to

Isaac Lewis Peet succeeded his father, Harvey P. Peet, as head of the New York School for the Deaf. In 1880, he was one of five Americans to attend the Congress of Milan. (See chapter 10.)

a special school by the time they reached age fourteen or fifteen, but it was even better if they could begin attending at eight or ten. The early home environment also was important. Parents should teach the children to write, and they should learn to communicate with their deaf children by means of natural gestures, then agreed-upon signs and fingerspelling. Finally, Peet had emphasized that deaf children should be taught to obey their parents like any other youngsters, but he cautioned that parents must make absolutely certain that they were understood. It would not do to punish a deaf child merely because communication had failed and he or she had not realized what behavior was acceptable.[5]

Evidence from family correspondence suggests that the Tillinghasts attempted to follow Peet's advice with respect to Thomas's communication, though perhaps not exactly as Peet had intended. For a short time in late 1841 and early 1842, apparently, they paid a Mrs. Ivey about nine dollars a month to board Thomas. Ivey was a teacher, but more importantly she had a deaf daughter, Eunice, who said that she would be "very happy to teach [the Tillinghasts'] deaf mute son," whom she would love "as her dear little brother." Specifically, she agreed to teach Thomas signs and fingerspelling. Thus Thomas had an opportunity at a very early age to interact with a grown and (presumably) educated deaf person.[6]

This was only a temporary expedient, however, and Thomas's maternal grandmother, Robina Norwood of Richmond, Virginia, urged the parents to put Thomas in a residential institution for deaf students. North Carolina did not have a state school for deaf students until 1845, though, so in May of 1842 Robina Norwood herself took Thomas to the Virginia School for the Deaf and the Blind in Staunton and enrolled him there. Thomas's experience at the school is chronicled in a series of letters that the Tillinghast family preserved, and they provide an excellent record of what it was like for a deaf child to attend a state residential school in the first half of the nineteenth century.

GOING TO SCHOOL

In one respect, the Virginia School was unusual. Opening in the fall of 1839, it was the first state institution to adopt the peculiar expedient—later copied by many states and still in practice in a few places

The Virginia School for the Deaf and the Blind in Staunton was one of many state residential schools patterned after the American School for the Deaf.

in the late twentieth century—of combining a school for deaf children with one for blind children.[7] In other respects, however, it was a typical early nineteenth-century residential school for deaf children.

Its governing body, called the Board of Visitors, turned to the older schools to find personnel to staff their new institution. They first attempted to hire Peet as principal, offering him the generous salary of $1,500 per year and a place to live. He declined, preferring New York City to Virginia's beautiful but remote Shenandoah Valley. The board then offered the position to a Hartford teacher, Joseph D. Tyler, who accepted.[8]

Tyler was a minister who had become hard-of-hearing himself as an adult. A graduate of Yale College and the Episcopal Theological Seminary of Virginia, in the fall of 1832 he began teaching at the American School and there remained until offered the principalship of the Virginia School in the fall of 1839. Immediately upon arriving in Virginia, he too turned back to the American School for assistance with the management of his new school. He tried to hire a deaf Hartford teacher and graduate, Edmund Booth, as the Virginia School's first instructor of deaf pupils. Booth, though, wished to move west, not south, and Tyler offered the position to another deaf person, Job

Turner.[9] A graduate of the American School, Turner accepted Tyler's offer and remained at the Virginia institution for nearly forty years, guaranteeing continuity from Hartford to the new school in Staunton.[10]

When young Thomas Tillinghast arrived in Staunton, Tyler put him under the charge of the school's matron, Margaret Eckridge. Since Thomas was a new pupil and unused to the regimen of life in a residential institution, Tyler did not at first require him to begin the academic program. Under Eckridge's watchful eyes he was allowed to adjust to his new surroundings by playing on the school grounds for a few days. This gradual adjustment worked well. Eckridge wrote to Mrs. Norwood on May 26 that her grandson cried only for a short while after she left him and now "appears perfectly contented and happy."[11]

Placed in the regular curriculum, Thomas continued to progress in the residential school environment. Principal Tyler reported "favorable accounts . . . in all respects of [Thomas's] health, behavior & improvement." Still, Thomas's unstructured childhood habits had to be suppressed to fit the rigid institutional existence residential schools necessarily demanded, and this caused some conflict with school authorities. Tyler reported that the eight-year-old from North Carolina at first showed a "boyish disinclination to the restraints of the school."[12] And the school did have restraints. Thomas wrote to his mother that all students followed a regular schedule. They arose from bed at four or five, probably depending upon the season, and then went to breakfast at six. This meal consisted of "butter, bread and coffee." Tyler then led the pupils in prayers at seven-thirty, followed by academic classes until one in the afternoon, with a half-hour recess from ten-thirty to eleven. A one-hour lunch break followed the morning classes. The afternoons were devoted to two and three-quarters hours of vocational education. Thomas mentioned that the Virginia School offered bookbinding, cabinet-making, and shoemaking, all of which were common in American schools for deaf students in the mid-nineteenth century. Supper followed a short recess, then more prayers, and finally the younger children had free time from seven to nine in the evening, when they went to bed. The older students had to be in bed by ten.[13]

Despite this rigid schedule, or perhaps because of its routine, within a few months Tyler wrote Mr. Tillinghast that his son's previous resistance to the school's regimen had "passed away & he has

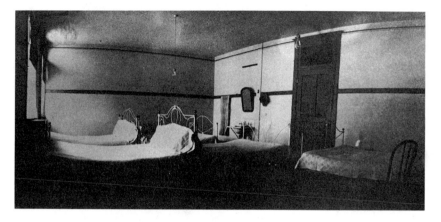

This dormitory room at the North Dakota School indicates the tight quarters and plain, unadorned style typical of state residential institutions, where discipline and conservative social behavior was stressed. Courtesy of the State Historical Society of North Dakota.

become quite docile." Yet his academic work was still weak, for Thomas was "young" and "unused to restraint." Nevertheless, Tyler emphasized, after six months at Staunton, Thomas had "gained a fondness for school & is acquiring habits of study which will carry him rapidly onward." He had even "learned to write quite a number of words & some little sentences."[14] As important as Thomas's learning was to the Tillinghasts, Tyler also recognized that Thomas's parents wanted to be certain that their son was receiving the care and concern young children needed.

Tyler's letters to the Tillinghasts stressed the paternal interest he showed for the school's charges. "Be assured," he wrote Mr. Tillinghast in November of 1842, "that your dear little boy will want for no attention in my power to bestow. My feelings toward all my pupils is, I think, warmer & more endearing than usual between teacher & pupil in ordinary schools, simply because my pupils are more helpless & more entirely dependent upon me."[15] The paternalism of Tyler's last few words—his stress upon deaf children's supposed helplessness—was characteristic of residential institutions in the mid-nineteenth century and was in this case perhaps compounded by the fact that Tyler was a minister who looked on his job as a calling or mission to assist those less fortunate than himself. In having a minister as its principal—as in many other respects—the Virginia School resembled its predecessor in Connecticut.

Tyler was a sensitive and perceptive principal. He appreciated parents' natural apprehensions about leaving their deaf children far from home in the hands of complete strangers. Tyler's letters to the Tillinghasts reflected his desire to help alleviate their distress and concern. He wrote comfortingly to them,

> I was a whole year separated 500 miles from my little children, & know well enough how to sympathize in the feelings of his [Thomas's] parents. Your anxiety must be very great & unintermitted, & I can say nothing perfectly to relieve your solicitude, but hope to allay it by leading you, if possible, to rely on all that I can do for the good of your absent child, & find some comfort in it. Please let me know how often to write.[16]

LEARNING

Thomas wrote his first letter home in November of 1842, about six months after he matriculated at the Virginia School and when he was nine years old. It was not entirely his own effort. Principal Tyler indicated that a teacher helped Thomas compose this first simple and direct attempt at written English communication with his parents. The letter read:

> my dear parents
> I am well. I am fat now. I hope that you are well. I love my mother & father. I wish to see my mother and father. I like to learn.
>
> your Affectionate son
Thomas Hooper Tillinghast[17]

The sentiments may have been genuine, or they may have been suggested by the adult who helped him compose the letter. In either case, they are precisely those that anxious parents would like to receive from their long-distant little boy.

Although the letter may seem a meager effort from a nine-year-old, it is important to recognize that Thomas entered the school completely ignorant of English. He was probably born deaf, and the short time he spent with Mrs. Ivey and her daughter was not sufficient to teach him anything more than the rudiments of sign language, if even that. The stilted and awkward English of the letter should not detract, either, from the fact that Thomas knew a great deal more than he was able to convey in this form.

The Virginia School recognized that the education of deaf children involved more than learning English. Deaf children were being prepared to go out into the world as independent and self-supporting individuals. Though all schools for deaf students tried to teach English and valued its attainment, this was not their only goal. They also wanted to be certain that their graduates had a marketable skill, one that did not require hearing to be practiced successfully. The students were expected to develop social skills, general knowledge, and religious awareness. Tyler stressed in a March 6, 1843, letter to the Tillinghasts that Thomas's achievement should not be evaluated solely on the basis of his English fluency.

Tyler's March 6 letter warned the Tillinghasts not to "mistake his knowledge of our language [written English] for the measure of his attainments." Sign language, Tyler wrote, enabled the school to acquaint Thomas "with an endless variety of things of which he knew nothing before." Though his writing was still poor, Tyler argued, Thomas "knows much which he cannot communicate to you yet in the English language." Tyler requested that the Tillinghast family help the school to communicate more effectively with Thomas by informing the school of the signs that Thomas had used before coming to school. In particular, the principal wished to know what signs his young pupil had used to designate various individuals within his family. Armed with this knowledge, Tyler would be able to interpret in signs the Tillinghasts' letters and "easily and distinctly make anything you wish to write to him known to him."[18]

The Virginia School's reliance on instruction in sign language produced results quickly. Two and one-half years after arriving at Staunton, Thomas Tillinghast could write grammatically correct English. More importantly, he was becoming aware of the larger world of knowledge. In an October 11, 1844, letter to his mother, the eleven-year-old boy even mentioned national politics, giving his opinion about the upcoming presidential election and the most controversial issue it involved, that is, the annexation of Texas. "I am," he wrote, "against Polk[,] Dallas and Texas." Thomas also was beginning to develop the rudiments of religious belief. "I am thankful to God," he told his mother. "God created the rain and the soil is fertile."[19]

Thomas's academic progress and social development were so rapid that Tyler even proposed taking him on a trip to North Carolina to exhibit his accomplishments to that state's legislature. The experience of Massieu and Clerc in England, and Clerc in New England, was now being replicated by Thomas Tillinghast in North Carolina. As those earlier pioneers had been used to demonstrate the effectiveness of the pedagogical models within which they learned, so Thomas was to be used. The Virginia School for the Deaf and the Blind, like the American School early in the nineteenth century, wished to become an area-wide school, serving not only Virginia but other southern states as well. Tyler wrote the Tillinghasts that "New England unites in supporting one Deafmute and one Blind Institution. New York has New Jersey united with her, & Pennsylvania [has] Maryland and Delaware." Thus Tyler planned to take Thomas with him to visit Raleigh, North Carolina, to convince that state not to establish its own school but to send North Carolina's deaf pupils to Virginia. Thomas would be the example of how successful that cooperation could be.[20]

PARENTAL GOALS

The Tillinghasts had clear goals for their deaf son. Their letters are free of any hope that Thomas would regain his hearing or that he would learn to speak and speechread. In the early nineteenth century, before some educators held out the promise of oral skills, parents seemed content to know that their deaf children would be capable of leading useful and satisfying lives.

Mr. Tillinghast was especially insistent that Thomas learn a "mechanical art." "Whatever course of life may be followed by you when you finish your studies," he wrote to his son, "the knowledge of a trade will be no disadvantage to you." The vocation he wished Thomas to pursue was bookbinding. Learning this trade would give his son something on which he could "rely to get a living" even if his property was lost. Without such a skill, he argued, Thomas might lose his independence "and have the mortification to be supported by our friends or come to absolute want." Moreover, he argued that Thomas might have to support his mother and younger siblings in the event of his, Mr. Tillinghast's, death.[21]

LEAVING SCHOOL

Thomas Tillinghast did not disappoint his father. After graduating with "high honors" from the Virginia Institution in 1850, he became a bookbinder and worked in that profession for several years in the

The North Carolina School for the Deaf and the Blind at Raleigh. David Ray Tillinghast and Thomas Tillinghast both taught here.

Fayetteville, North Carolina, area. After the Civil War the economy was depressed, however, and he turned to another occupation, one common to the best graduates of residential schools until late in the nineteenth century. In 1874 Thomas Tillinghast joined his deaf brother, David Ray Tillinghast, as a teacher in the North Carolina Institution for the Deaf and Dumb in Raleigh and later in the Morganton Institution.[22]

David had not followed in his brother's footsteps. Born in 1841—apparently with normal hearing—he became deaf as a child. When he was twelve years old, his parents sent him to the New York Institution rather than to Virginia for his education. After graduating and teaching at his alma mater for six years, in 1868 he joined the teaching faculty at Raleigh. He thus began a career that lasted well into the twentieth century (he was over one hundred years old when he died) and started a Tillinghast tradition in deaf education. Other Tillinghasts would become teachers and administrators in schools for deaf children throughout the United States, and one son of David Tillinghast even headed an institution for deaf students in Ireland.[23]

Joseph A. Tillinghast, son of David Tillinghast, was a member of the second generation of Tillinghasts to be teachers and administrators in schools for deaf children.

That Thomas and David Tillinghast graduated from state residential schools for deaf students and then returned to them for employment is not surprising. They were evidently precocious students, and like other deaf people who attended residential schools, they returned to them to find companionship, jobs appropriate to their level of education, and a culture based on the common language of signs. Many alumni of deaf institutions in nineteenth-century America,

Edward W. Tillinghast, a hearing grandson of David Ray Tillinghast, was an administrator at the Arizona School for the Deaf. He and his sister, Hilda Tillinghast Williams, represented the third generation of Tillinghasts involved in deaf education.

*A teacher of deaf students, Hilda
Tillinghast in 1937 married Boyce R.
Williams, the deaf man most responsible for
vocational rehabilitation programs for deaf
Americans in the twentieth century.*

who ironically were often better educated than their parents—as Mr.
Tillinghast perceptively noted when he attended Thomas's graduation
in 1850—founded America's deaf community by reentering as adults
the environment they enjoyed as students. Those who did not become teachers, however, sought other ways to recreate the sense of
fellowship and shared experience that marked their school years.

6

A Deaf State

Minorities often believe their culture will flourish and their aspirations will be achieved if they separate themselves politically and geographically from the majority. Thus, in the early nineteenth century, Latter Day Saints fled to the remote deserts of Utah, where they hoped to develop unique social and political structures based on their particular needs and beliefs, away from the ridicule and persecution of non-Mormons.[1] Similarly, at an earlier period in American history English Puritans left their homes and emigrated to North America to establish an exclusive community, one for them alone.[2] In the early twentieth century many black Americans dreamed of leaving the white-dominated United States and creating a black nation of their own in Africa.[3]

Deaf Americans resemble blacks and other minorities in many respects, one of which is their desire to free themselves from the limitations imposed on them by the majority. Like Latter Day Saints, Puritans, and blacks, some deaf people have considered establishing their own political unit, under their own control, and separate from all hearing influences. Douglas Bullard's 1985 novel *Islay* is a humorous expression of this often-discussed idea.[4] A serious discussion of a separate commonwealth for deaf people, however, occurred in the mid-nineteenth century.

The timing is not surprising. As nineteenth-century residential institutions brought deaf individuals together and initiated the creation of a deaf culture, deaf people recognized that they were often happiest and most successful among persons who shared their language and perspective. A few academically talented individuals, like the Tillinghast brothers, satisfied their need to be among their deaf fellows by taking jobs in residential schools. There they could interact with other deaf adults and with deaf children who would perpetuate evolving deaf mores. Within the institutions they were relatively free from pressure to conform to the linguistic demands typically placed on them by the hearing and speaking majority of Americans, and they could develop useful, satisfying, and fairly lucrative careers. Teaching in the residential institutions was not an option open to all deaf Americans, however, and for some of them—such as the remarkable John J. Flournoy—the frustrations of daily life in a hearing world led to plans for a deaf state in the American West.

JOHN J. FLOURNOY

No more bizarre individual than John Jacobus Flournoy is to be found in the history of deaf Americans. One of two deaf sons of a wealthy Georgia slaveholder, Flournoy briefly attended the American School in Connecticut and the University of Georgia. He also was an inmate in the South Carolina state mental institution, to which he first committed himself and from which he later released himself. Flournoy rarely cut his hair or his beard. He wore a rubber raincoat in all seasons, and he rode about on a small donkey. A prolific letter writer, he wrote prose so convoluted and wordy that it is nearly incomprehensible. Yet Flournoy was not merely an eccentric; he encouraged the establishment of the Georgia School for the Deaf and argued for other measures to assist deaf people. Most importantly, he articulated in a public forum the private feelings of at least some other deaf Americans in the mid-nineteenth century.

In 1855 Flournoy sent a circular to deaf Americans and Europeans complaining that deaf people had suffered "rejections and consignments to inferior places." He wrote from personal experience. Several times Flournoy had sought government positions and had been rejected. Although he was independently wealthy and therefore did not need the income of a government career, he sought the status and power such a job would bestow. His circular argued that the hearing majority had not allowed deaf people to demonstrate their capacity for high-level jobs, particularly in government. To overcome this situation, he suggested that members of the deaf community who so desired might think about choosing a place to settle in the American

West and then move there and assume all governing responsibilities. In December of 1855 he broached this idea with William W. Turner, a hearing man and one of his former teachers at the American School.[5]

Turner was sympathetic yet skeptical. "Your plan is beautiful in theory," he wrote to Flournoy. "That educated deaf-mutes are capable of self-government and of managing the affairs of a State of their own, there can be no doubt." He went on to say that deaf people would "be more favorably situated in such a community" for their social activities, civil and religious privileges, and self-improvement. The practical problems, however, seemed overwhelming to Turner.[6]

Two obvious difficulties presented themselves. First, Turner argued that it would be impossible to convince deaf people to leave the communities in which they already were established. They had friends, relatives, homes, and jobs in their present locations. Deaf people, Turner wrote, would be "unwilling to break the endearing ties which bind them to these objects of their affection." A second problem was children. "How will you keep it [your deaf state] a mute community?" Turner asked. "It has been found by careful examination of facts, that only one in twenty children of deaf-mute parents is deaf and dumb." The only possible solution, he suggested, was to force hearing children to emigrate from the state, and this he regarded as obviously unsatisfactory.

Turner then developed another argument, one that provoked

William W. Turner, a hearing minister and teacher at the American School for the Deaf, advised John J. Flournoy that his idea of developing a separate state for deaf people was unnecessary and impractical.

scorn from Flournoy because of its assumption that deaf people were inherently limited in what they could achieve.

> You would not think it wise [Turner insisted] to give the command of any army to a blind man. The want of sight would utterly disqualify him for the post. For a similar reason, you would not send a deaf and dumb man to Congress or to the Legislature of a State; not for the reason that he was deficient in intelligence and education, but because his want of hearing and speech unfits him for the place.[7]

Turner's criticism contained one further point. He disagreed with Flournoy's assessment that hearing people regarded well-educated deaf people as "unworthy of any place of profit, influence or authority." To the contrary, argued Turner—who was hearing himself—"There is [sic], I am sure, nothing but feelings of kindness entertained and expressed by" hearing persons toward those who are deaf. Flournoy needed to accept the fact, Turner concluded, "that in a speaking and hearing community, as business is now conducted, there are many offices and positions which a deaf-mute can not properly occupy, owing to the deprivation of faculties essential to the performance of their appropriate duties." In Turner's view this was not the result of "prejudice or injustice"; it was merely reality.[8]

Flournoy responded to Turner with characteristic emotion, tangled syntax, and powerful insight. "The old cry about the incapacity of men's minds from physical disabilities," he insisted, "I think it were time, now in this intelligent age, to *explode!*" More calmly, he asserted that lame, blind, or deaf men certainly were not ever viewed as useless when their labor was needed. From the perceptive realization that handicapped people (and, he might have added, women and minorities) were exploited whenever doing so met the needs of those with power, he jumped to the illogical conclusion that, therefore, Turner's argument that deaf people could not hold certain positions was false.[9]

Whatever the weakness of this part of Flournoy's argument, he had expressed important ideas. He implied that deaf people shared certain characteristics with other disabled persons. In this realization he was far ahead of his time. It was not until after World War II that the leadership of the American deaf community would work to ally itself with other disabled people to struggle for civil rights. Flournoy was sufficiently well educated and creative also to perceive that disability was not an absolute characteristic, that it was socially defined. Flournoy recognized that if dominant groups needed handicapped people, then they were viewed as useful; if they did not need them, then they were said to have limited capacity.

Flournoy's rebuttals to Turner's practical objections were less satisfactory. He simply denied Turner's assertion that deaf people would not be willing to leave their homes, jobs, and friends to emigrate. The key, he argued, was whether they would be allowed absolute power within their own state. A true deaf community, he insisted, where all offices would be held by deaf persons and where no one else could live, "would easily draw mute recipients . . . from all sections" of the United States. As to the question of children, Flournoy, who was alienated from his own hearing offspring, simply responded, "If our children hear, let them go to other states." Even in hearing communities, he concluded, children do not stay with their parents forever.

Flournoy denied Turner's confident assertion that most hearing people look favorably upon deaf people. He accused hearing people of prejudice against those who could not hear and wrote that "sometimes" hearing people deprived deaf people their rightful positions out of "malignance." In his home region, the South, he argued that deaf people were "contemned, spurned, degraded and abhorred" by "the auricular," that is, by those who could hear.[10]

If the Flournoy–Turner argument had remained confined to these two individuals, it could be ignored as a merely personal disagreement among two people, one a hearing person who had never experienced the consequences of deafness and the other a most peculiar and bitter deaf man. What makes it important, though, is that it did not remain confined to these two people. Flournoy's suggestion of a deaf commonwealth raised issues of such importance and such strong feeling in the mid-nineteenth century that it attracted attention throughout the United States. When the exchange of letters between Flournoy and Turner was published in the *American Annals of the Deaf*, they aroused a torrent of comment from deaf and hearing people. Among the former, one of the most formidable critics of the deaf commonwealth idea was Edmund Booth.

Booth graduated from the American School, taught there briefly, and then moved west, where he became a model of the successful nineteenth-century American pioneer. Like most people on the frontier, he dabbled in several enterprises before settling on one that served him well. He farmed in Iowa for a short time and there held several minor government positions. Later he joined the California gold rush. Although he did not become wealthy in California's

One of Flournoy's strongest critics in the deaf community was Edmund Booth of Iowa. A successful newspaper editor, Booth believed that deaf people profitted from association with hearing persons.

gold fields, he acquired enough money to return to Iowa and purchase a newspaper, which he edited and owned for the rest of his life. While in Iowa he lobbied for a state school for deaf children and wrote strongly abolitionist editorials. In 1880 he chaired the Cincinnati meeting that established the National Association of the Deaf.[11]

Unlike Flournoy, Booth felt neither alienation nor oppression. He functioned easily and comfortably among hearing people, despite blindness in one eye and profound deafness. Yet he did not avoid contact with deaf people, either. He married one of his former students from the American School, Mary Ann Walworth; took a deaf man with him to California; there befriended other deaf people; and played an active role in local and national deaf affairs after he returned to Iowa.[12] Completely and happily bi-cultural, Booth was wary of the results of creating a totally deaf community.

He wrote to Flournoy that a deaf commonwealth would tend to lower the intellectual achievements of its inhabitants. Only a few deaf people were well educated, Booth argued; the rest were "half-educated," "non-readers and frivolous." Booth feared that the demand for equality among these disparate individuals would "keep the more sensible from joining such a community." It was better, Booth believed, to keep deaf people scattered among "their hearing associates, [because] in such situations they are compelled to *read* and *write*, and thus keep their minds under the educational process through life."[13] Booth was not the only deaf critic who believed that deaf persons needed the cultural stimulation of living among hearing people.

John Carlin expressed a similar concern, though he did so much more cynically. A graduate of the Pennsylvania Institution for the Deaf, sometime teacher and artist, Carlin was no friend of sign language. He ridiculed Flournoy's deaf state, recommending for it the names "Deaf-Mutia" or "Gesturia." Suggesting that is was nothing but a "castle in the air," he insisted that deaf people would never have the financial strength, patience, perseverance, or diligence necessary to make Flournoy's plan succeed. Denigrating his deaf fellows, he wrote,

> It must be borne in mind that nine-tenths of the whole deaf-mute community in this country can not raise up the wind so as to swell the flapping sails of Mr. Flournoy's scheme; besides, it is a well known fact that the majority of them show little decision of purpose in any enterprise whatever.

Further showing his contempt for deaf Americans, he stated that he preferred to remain among hearing people, "whose superior knowledge of the English language benefits my mind far more than would the perpetual gestures" of the inhabitants of "Gesturia."[14]

Carlin voiced an extreme position. A snob and a frustrated man, he articulated the position that deaf culture was inferior. Based on a nonspoken language, it could not, he believed, elevate the mind or allow its users to achieve greatness in the sciences, art, or literature. Ironically, though, Carlin married a deaf woman and spent most of his life among deaf people, working for their benefit and constantly exhorting them to acquire English language skills and to strive to succeed as did hearing people.[15] Later he would argue in favor of establishing an institution of higher education for deaf individuals, and he received the first honorary degree awarded by Gallaudet College.[16]

In sharp contrast to the haughty and arrogant Carlin, P. H. Confer of Indiana warmly embraced Flournoy's scheme. Confer was a sad individual whose letter to the *American Annals of the Deaf* indicated just how lonely a deaf person, even a relatively wealthy deaf person, could be. Twenty-four years old, single, deaf since age ten, and without siblings or parents, he wrote, pitifully, "I am alone." He owned an Indiana farm that he had inherited from his parents, and he felt despised by hearing people. "I am for a place where all my deaf-mute brethren could live and be happy," he continued. This was not possible among those who hear, for deaf people could not converse with them and thus were made to look like fools. With others who were deaf, everyone would be equal and communication easy and natural. Confer even offered $5,000 of his own money to assist in the establishment of a deaf commonwealth. Despite his wealth—he owned a farm worth $18,000 and held $2,000 in cash—"I am not happy," he concluded, "with the present condition of the deaf and dumb."[17] Confer was a deaf person who had not found a deaf community. Thus he hoped that in the West one might be created so that he would no longer be alone and have to suffer the humiliation of his deafness.

REJECTION

In 1858 Laurent Clerc commented on the issue of an exclusively deaf state. The occasion was the third meeting of the New England Gallaudet Association of Deaf-Mutes, the first formal organization established by and for deaf Americans. Clerc's opinion was held in high regard. Not only was he the most famous and most highly respected deaf person in nineteenth-century America, he also was widely considered to be the person who first proposed that deaf people segregate themselves from the hearing majority by moving, as a group, to a state of their own.

By 1858, though, Clerc was a relatively satisfied seventy-two-year-old man. Living in comfort in his adopted Hartford, Connecticut, where he had converted to the Episcopalianism of the city's upper class and where he and his wife had raised a large family of hearing children, his response to Flournoy's plan was no surprise. He said that his earlier beliefs had been misunderstood. He had never supported the idea of a state exclusively for deaf people. Early in the history of the American School he had suggested that some of the Alabama land that the federal government had given to the school might be used as a "headquarters" for the deaf and dumb. This did not imply the creation of a deaf state, Clerc insisted, for that was an embellishment of Flournoy's.

Clerc stated further that he saw many practical difficulties with Flournoy's conception. He believed, for example, that "exclusiveness" was undesirable, for it was convenient to have hearing people around in case of sickness or fire. In addition, he thought that any state for deaf people alone would have to be so remote from other settled areas that it would be in constant danger of aggression from hostile persons—presumably meaning Indians or citizens of other countries. Clerc thought Flournoy's plan "the offspring of a disordered imagination," and he asked the convention whether the members felt themselves despised or maltreated. When they answered no, he asked if they wished to live separately in a deaf and dumb community or if they wished to remain mixed in the general population of people who hear and speak. They responded as he wished, saying that they preferred their present circumstances.[18]

Two hearing ministers present at the convention, the Reverend Thomas Gallaudet, the son of Thomas Hopkins Gallaudet, and the Reverend W. W. Turner from the American School, added their support to Clerc's theme. They too suggested that Flournoy's ideas were not representative of those of most deaf people. Gallaudet, speaking with the authority of a person with a deaf wife and a deaf mother, said the Georgian's thoughts represented a "morbid state of feeling," and Turner said Flournoy's attitude toward the hearing community rested "on no foundation whatever." Indeed, Turner concluded, what difference did it make how deaf people were viewed in the present world, since in the hereafter all persons—deaf and hearing—stood an equal chance of receiving justice and mercy?[19]

Most recorded reaction to Flournoy's idea was negative, and perhaps his perception of the reality faced by deaf people was colored by his particular circumstances. Flournoy lived most of his life in the pre–Civil War South. On a daily basis he was exposed to a rigid society characterized by the effects of slavery and dominated by a narrow, self-conscious, and defensive planter class. Where Booth had been able to serve in government in the fluid and egalitarian conditions of frontier Iowa, Flournoy had been thwarted by the inflexibility of his older region.

There is, however, another possible explanation of the cool reaction to Flournoy's plan. The people who wrote letters to the *American Annals of the Deaf*—and most of the individuals who attended the meetings of the New England Gallaudet Association—were successful deaf people. They were the ones who had graduated from residential schools, often compiling excellent academic records. They did not struggle with English or depend totally on sign language to communicate their thoughts. Even Flournoy's strongest supporter, Confer, had become deafened at age ten and therefore presumably was comfortable with spoken and written English. Some had deaf relatives and thus enjoyed close association with others who shared their needs. Those in the Gallaudet Association, all New Englanders and all alumni of the American School, also had the advantage of regular contact with other deaf people. In the school they had established social ties that they continued throughout their lives in the relatively compact New England area. The less articulate, those who were born deaf and who grew up without education and without the benefit of deaf family, were not heard from. Feeling more acutely the frustrations voiced by Flournoy, they might have voted differently than did Booth, Carlin, and the other intellectual leaders of deaf America.[20]

THE ENGLISH EXPERIENCE

Americans were not alone in imagining a remote western utopia for people who could not hear. Late in the nineteenth century a scheme somewhat parallel to Flournoy's developed in England. That country had no uncultivated public land that deaf people might be able to colonize, but huge, largely unpopulated, Canada did.

Jane Elizabeth Groom, a hard-of-hearing graduate of the Manchester School for the Deaf in England, proposed in the early 1880s that deaf Londoners be settled in Canada's Manitoba Province. "I have noticed so much distress amongst the deaf and dumb," she wrote, "that I feel perfectly sad at witnessing it, and I am sure that nothing can be done for them here to establish them satisfactorily." Newspaper articles and pamphlets appeared in London urging donations toward this cause.[21] One such pamphlet noted that deaf people suffered terrible poverty in London because they were unable to compete with hearing people in the tight labor market of their home country. Thus, Groom suggested, "I desire that a grant of land be made by Her Majesty's Government in Canada for the deaf and dumb and their families, so that they may be afforded the opportunity of being healthy, bright, useful and happy without being dependent."[22]

In important respects, Groom's appeal was different from Flournoy's. The Englishwoman never anticipated a community or commonwealth composed exclusively of deaf individuals. Furthermore, where Flournoy had made his argument to deaf people, since they were the ones who would move, Groom appealed to hearing people, that is, to those with the financial and political means to make her plan a success. Flournoy based his arguments on the need for deaf people to be by themselves, in complete control of their destiny. Groom based hers on the popular sentiment that people should support themselves economically and that those who were deaf could do so only where they would face little economic competition from hearing people, such as in the remote wilds of Northwest Canada on unsettled land or in small towns with labor shortages. In short, Groom's scheme was a plan of welfare, whereas Flournoy's was a demand for self-determination for a confident and educated minority group.

Groom's plan had some success, but not on the scale she envisaged. In 1884 and 1885 she took groups of deaf people to the Canadian Immigration Station at Winnipeg. From that location most of them quickly gained employment on farms and in the farming communities of western Canada. These deaf pioneers then saved money to bring their parents and other relatives out to join them.[23]

What gives Groom's plan its historical importance is the contrast it presents between a poverty-stricken and dependent minority of deaf people in England, on the one hand, and an aggressive, articulate, argumentative American deaf community on the other. By the time that Groom was making her pathetic plea for assistance for England's downtrodden deaf people, deaf Americans, by contrast, already had established their own national organization (the National Association of the Deaf) and were beginning to graduate from their own college, today's Gallaudet University.

7

A College

By 1857 the United States boasted nineteen residential schools for deaf students. Most were in the eastern half of the country, but the states of Missouri, Iowa, Louisiana, and Texas—all west of the Mississippi River—also had recognized the needs of their deaf children and opened schools.[1] In some respects, each school was different. Levels of state support varied, as did the number of pupils enrolled and the quality of instruction and administration. In terms of their main institutional goals, however, all American schools for deaf students resembled each other.

The faculty and administration from Hartford, Connecticut, to Austin, Texas, and at every residential school in between, focused on preparing their charges to become working members of society immediately upon graduation. Though this goal often was not met, it nevertheless determined the curriculum students followed and defined the expectations for deaf pupils. Typically, academic work was limited to the elementary "three r's"—reading, writing, and arithmetic. In the larger schools, such as those of New York, Connecticut, and Pennsylvania, a superficial introduction to disciplines like history, philosophy, and literature was available to the most successful students, but the emphasis was on vocational training: printing, shoemaking, and carpentry for boys and sewing for girls.[2]

Thus in the middle of the nineteenth century the horizons of most deaf children were strictly limited. They would not become professionals or experience significant social mobility. Unless they came from wealthy families or had the academic ability and good fortune to acquire teaching positions in schools for deaf children, most could not aspire even to middle-class life. At best, they were trained to be skilled laborers.

In this respect, however, there was nothing unusual about the fate of deaf boys and girls. Working-class children who attended American public schools before the Civil War were similarly limited to elementary subjects and vocational preparation.[3] A few hearing children from wealthy families attended private academies, where they received classical educations and then went on to college, but they were a small minority. In those days before the Morrill Act and the establishment of the great public universities, the land-grant institutions of the late nineteenth century, college was too expensive and too impractical for most students. It was widely assumed that, beyond reading, writing, arithmetic, and perhaps a touch of history, education was a waste of resources for individuals who would become farmers, housewives, manual laborers, or artisans anyway. Given this environment, it is therefore surprising that the idea of a college for deaf people suddenly surfaced in the 1850s and became a reality in the 1860s.

The Collegiate Department of the Columbia Institution for the Deaf and Dumb opened in 1864. Later renamed in honor of Thomas Hopkins Gallaudet, this college became—and remained for more than

Gallaudet College ca. 1892.

one hundred years—the only institution of its kind in the world.[4] It also became the finishing school for most of the men and women who shaped America's deaf community in the late nineteenth and twentieth centuries. Although a handful of deaf people, generally from affluent families, graduated from other universities, those who identified with the deaf community and supplied its leadership were products of the Gallaudet experience.[5]

The federal government chartered and funded Gallaudet College, establishing a precedent for its relations with Howard University. Federal support made it a national institution; thus Gallaudet was free to draw together the brightest and most ambitious deaf students from throughout the United States. On its Kendall Green campus in Washington, D.C., they came to know each other; soon they constituted a self-appointed deaf cultural elite. Since the late nineteenth century, Gallaudet graduates have dominated the national deaf organizations, controlled important periodicals, and supplied most of America's deaf teachers.

With the founding of Gallaudet College, deaf Americans leapt far beyond their counterparts in other nations. Those who showed academic ability could attend college at a time when few hearing Americans had even a secondary school education. Ironically, and owing to the low cost of their federally subsidized education, many deaf children became the first persons in their families to experience

Edward Allen Fay was the first vice-president of Gallaudet College and editor of the American Annals of the Deaf *for nearly fifty years. A hearing man who grew up on the campus of the Michigan School for the Deaf, he supported the right of deaf people to be educated by means of sign language.*

college. Gallaudet's success in this bold experiment demonstrated that deaf individuals did not have to be manual laborers, that they had the intellectual skills necessary for professional occupations.

Gallaudet College had a further important impact on the American deaf community. From its inception, the college based all of its instruction on sign language. Its president for more than fifty years, Edward Miner Gallaudet, learned sign language from his famous father and from his deaf mother, and he revered it always. The college's first vice president, Edward Allen Fay, who served nearly as long as Gallaudet, grew up on the campus of the Michigan School for the Deaf, where his father was superintendent.[6] Fay, too, was both a master of American Sign Language and a fervent advocate of its use.[7] Deaf faculty, present from the earliest years, also strengthened the college's commitment to the language of deaf America.[8] During the late nineteenth and early twentieth centuries, when the tides of oralism washed over and changed fundamentally most schools for deaf pupils, Gallaudet College remained a solid and powerful bastion of sign language.

ORIGINS

The first public discussion of a college for deaf people appeared in the *American Annals of the Deaf* in 1851. Jacob Van Nostrand, a hearing teacher at the New York Institution, stated the case boldly.

John B. Hotchkiss, a graduate of the American School for the Deaf and Gallaudet College, in 1869 became the college's first deaf teacher. His fields were history and English.

Amos G. Draper was the second deaf teacher at Gallaudet College. A graduate of the American School for the Deaf, he worked as a printer for several years before enrolling at Gallaudet in 1872. He taught mathematics and Latin.

Something must be done. Something that shall open to the mind of the deaf mute a wider range in the fields of knowledge than he has heretofore enjoyed; something to animate and excite him in the pursuit of knowledge, until he can take his place among the scholars and sages of the world.[9]

Van Nostrand did not mean to criticize the residential schools or their programs. Rather, he argued that they had reached a plateau in their development. He wrote that deaf students did not extend themselves, did not exert all their efforts toward academic success because they realized that their horizons were limited. After residential school, there were no more possibilities for continued intellectual growth and no incentives for further scholastic pursuit. The limited opportunities for learning in the residential schools, he believed, created a "chain" that bound deaf Americans "to mere physical labors and the common drudgeries of life." The obvious question, then, was "what shall be done, and how shall it be done?"[10]

Van Nostrand did not have the vision to recommend the creation of a college, but he did suggest something very close to it. He wrote that institutions should select a few students with the greatest language proficiency and strongest commitment to scholarship and "offer them the privilege of a still further course of one or two years' instruction." This instruction would be radically different from that pursued previously. Instead of the three r's and vocational training, the students would follow a curriculum of "mental and moral philosophy, natural history, mathematics and natural philosophy, history and English literature; in short, with the exception of the dead languages, all the studies usually pursued in higher academies or even in colleges."

Van Nostrand's special course also would be taught differently than the classes students were used to. It would have "lectures and interlocutory examinations." The teachers and pupils would not spend their time on language work, reviewing the "principles of construction, or the illustration of [English] words"; they would concentrate on the "subject matter at hand," that is, the content of the disciplines to which they were being introduced. The educational program Van Nostrand proposed would differ from those of hearing academies and colleges only in one respect—all instruction would be "carried on in the language of signs instead of [in] oral language."[11]

This program, Van Nostrand believed, would be useful to all deaf students, even those who would never be able to enter it. Its effect would be to raise the general level of academic achievement throughout the institutions. "Fix a limit," Van Nostrand argued, "beyond which none may pass and soon even that limit will not be reached by any." Create the possibility of students going beyond that limit, however, and achievement would "be an object of ambition to all."[12] In short, if students knew that there was a possibility of extending their scholastic development beyond the confines of the regular program of the residential institutions, they would work harder, and the general achievement of all would be affected.

John Carlin agreed. The artist, critic of Flournoy, and articulate spokesman for educated deaf Americans responded to Van Nostrand in the very next issue of the *Annals*. He argued that lack of a collegiate experience had caused "many promising deaf mutes' minds . . . to wither and droop into obscurity." Worse, these individuals had "been compelled to earn a livelihood by common manual labors" that were incongruous "with the elevated character of their minds."[13] Carlin recognized that school curricula that limited deaf children to elementary education and vocational training doomed them to working-class lives and foreclosed the development of a comfortable deaf middle class. Characteristically, Carlin also criticized Van Nostrand's plan. He said that it was too limited, that the subjects Van Nostrand recommended needed more than a two-year's course for their completion.[14]

It was not until 1854, however, that Carlin developed a full argument in favor of a college for deaf students, not merely the advanced

An artist, teacher, critic of signs, and graduate of the Pennsylvania Institution for the Deaf, John Carlin in the 1850s argued for the establishment of a college for deaf Americans. In 1864 he received Gallaudet College's first honorary degree.

JOHN CARLIN.

courses that Van Nostrand had suggested. Writing again in the *Annals*, Carlin proposed that the question "Is a college absolutely necessary for gifted mutes?" become the subject of a debate in the *Annals* and at the next convention of the New England Gallaudet Association of Deaf-Mutes.[15] He argued that, sadly, "deaf mutes have no finished scholars of their own to boast of, while the speaking community present to our mental vision an imposing array of scholars." The reason for this, he believed, was simply that deaf people "have no universities, colleges, high schools or lyceums of their own" that would elevate their scholastic achievements to those of hearing persons.[16]

Carlin also argued that his own research had shown that this deplorable situation did not have to continue. Since the publication of Van Nostrand's original article, Carlin wrote, he had made a "careful and impartial investigation" of the progress made by pupils in the "High Class" established by Isaac Lewis Peet at the New York Institution and a similar class at the American School at Hartford. In one and one-half years, pupils in these special classes had made "prodigious strides" in "rhetoric, astronomy, chemistry, the Old Testament . . . history, geography, and algebra." Nevertheless, he continued, the work of these pupils was but a "step" toward college, not a substitute for it.[17]

Carlin concluded his proposal by advancing four points. He first stated that it was reasonable to establish one college for "promising mutes and semi-mutes [persons deafened after learning speech]" since there were many colleges and universities for hearing people, and the former had "a just claim" to the superior education of the latter. His second point stressed the abilities of deaf people. Carlin argued that deaf people might not be equal to speaking people in "the correctness and elegance of their language," but there was sufficient precedent to demonstrate that they were capable of first-rate scholarship. To support this point, he mentioned several examples of well-known deaf men, including the English linguist and Bible scholar John Kitto; Jean-Ferdinand Berthier, the French teacher and writer; the American poet James Nack; and the celebrated Laurent Clerc.[18] All of these, Carlin emphasized, "have never been educated at colleges." A national college for deaf people, Carlin argued in his third point, would be a nursery to produce deaf professionals—"especially civil engineers, physicians, surgeons, lawyers and statesmen"—and restore these people to society, "from which they have been isolated" because of "their misfortune" and "the poverty of their minds." Finally, Carlin appealed to the patriotism of the young and vigorously growing nation. Such a college would, he wrote with pardonable hyperbole, "add fresh luster to the halo of glory encircling our blessed republic."[19]

Carlin achieved a modicum of glory himself when he received the first honorary degree of the college he envisioned and pleaded for. The person most responsible for bringing that vision to fruition, however, was Edward Miner Gallaudet.

EDWARD MINER GALLAUDET

Born in 1837, the youngest of eight children of Sophia Fowler and Thomas Hopkins Gallaudet, the youthful Edward Miner seemed an unlikely person to found a college. He wished to go into business and to earn a quick fortune. At the age of fourteen, immediately after completing high school and shortly after his father died, Gallaudet became a clerk in the Phoenix Bank of Hartford. When the clerkship bored him, he quit and enrolled in Trinity College in Hartford. In 1855, while still a student at Trinity, he accepted a teaching position at the American School, the school his father and Laurent Clerc had established thirty-eight years earlier.[20]

Yet Gallaudet was not entirely happy there, either. He wrote later that he had wanted to do something more for deaf people "than merely to teach them or become the principal of a school." When a fellow teacher, Jared A. Ayres, mentioned to Gallaudet that the idea of a college for deaf pupils had been discussed, he was attracted to the possibility. Neither Gallaudet nor Ayres, though, had any notion of how to go about establishing such an institution unless "a millionaire could be found to endow it."[21] Restless and unsatisfied with his situation at the American School, Gallaudet considered following the footsteps of his father and older brother by entering the ministry, with hopes of becoming a missionary in China. That idea, too, collapsed for lack of money, and Gallaudet once more thought of going into business. In the spring of 1857 he resigned his teaching job at Hartford, accepted a financially attractive position in a Chicago bank, and prepared to leave Hartford.[22]

Gallaudet never went to Chicago or back into the banking business. Before departing for the Midwest, he had an extraordinary bit of good luck. He received a letter from Amos Kendall that stirred his ambition and recalled his conversations with Ayres; thus, by coincidence, the history of deaf Americans was forever altered.

Kendall was a wealthy Washingtonian and philanthropist. Originally a newspaper editor, he had been an early political advisor to Andrew Jackson. When Jackson won the presidency in 1828 Kendall became one of his influential friends known as the "kitchen cabinet."[23] Later Jackson rewarded Kendall for his loyal support by naming him postmaster general of the United States, a position he also

Amos Kendall was a wealthy Washington philanthropist who donated the land that became Kendall Green, the home of Gallaudet College, and who hired Edward Miner Gallaudet to head the Columbia Institution for the Deaf and Dumb and the Blind.

held in the presidency of Jackson's hand-picked successor, Martin Van Buren.[24] After his political career, Kendall made a fortune through investments in the telegraph, invented by his friend Samuel F. B. Morse. Although he had no previous interest in deaf people or familiarity with them, a complex series of historical accidents led him to become the legal guardian of five deaf orphans. In 1857 he decided to establish a school for them—and for blind children—in the District of Columbia, and to this end he sought a superintendent who could provide the expertise he did not have.

Kendall turned to Harvey P. Peet, the venerable head of the New York Institution, for advice. Kendall wanted a teacher who was familiar with deaf education, but he was especially interested in selecting an individual who did not have a family to support and thus could be hired for a low salary and would not require large living accommodations on the school grounds. Peet recommended that Kendall talk with Gallaudet.[25]

Although Gallaudet was very young to be a superintendent—only twenty years old—Peet argued that he might be convinced to bring his deaf mother with him. She could serve as the school's matron and would, in Kendall's words to Gallaudet, "assist you by her counsel and efforts." In the mid-nineteenth century, an unmarried young man would not normally have been considered suitable for a position involving the superintendence of children in a residential setting, but the presence of Gallaudet's mother overcame that objection. Kendall, therefore, decided to accept Peet's recommendation to approach Gallaudet.[26]

A knowledgeable and influential man, Kendall made significant steps toward the founding of his school even before he contacted Gallaudet. He persuaded Congress to incorporate in the District of Columbia an "Institution for the instruction of the Deaf and Dumb and the Blind." He also convinced Congress to allocate $150 per year for "every indigent [deaf or blind] pupil belonging to the District" and to permit the school to accept students from all parts of the United States. In this way, Kendall laid the national foundation upon which the college's ultimate success would depend. On May 14, 1857, he wrote to Gallaudet proposing that the two meet to discuss the possibility of Gallaudet's becoming, with his mother's assistance, the institution's superintendent.[27]

Gallaudet was pleased with the proposal yet cautious. He discussed the matter with Ayres, and both concluded that this might be

Sophia Fowler was the fifteenth student enrolled at the American School for the Deaf. She married Thomas Hopkins Gallaudet, and in 1857 she joined her son, Edward Miner Gallaudet, on Kendall Green, where she became the first matron of Kendall School.

the opportunity they had dreamed about previously of founding a college for deaf Americans.[28] Gallaudet wrote back to Kendall on May 18, but he said nothing about a college. Instead, he told Kendall the idea of "enlightening the minds of Deaf-Mutes . . . occupies a warm place in my heart." He went on to say "my inclinations lead me to embrace the opportunity offered and to labor zealously to the extent of my strength and ability." Still, he requested specific details about

Edward Miner Gallaudet was only twenty years old when he was hired as superintendent of the Columbia Institution and boldly proposed the establishment of a college for deaf people.

salary, the present conditions of the school, and its prospects for the future. Gallaudet concluded by suggesting that he and Kendall meet in New York or Hartford to discuss these matters.[29]

Subsequently, Kendall invited Gallaudet to visit him in Washington. There they discussed each other's ideas, and Gallaudet raised the possibility of creating a college in addition to the residential school Kendall had proposed. Gallaudet later recounted that meeting.

> I unfolded to him [Kendall] my plans for a college and said that if he and his associates . . . would support me in these plans, I would accept their offer. They met my overtures with alacrity, pleased with the idea of having what they conceived of as no more than a small local school, grow ultimately into an institution of national importance and influence.[30]

THE COLLEGE

Gallaudet's first priority was to establish the residential school on a firm basis. To this end he brought in James Denison, a deaf teacher at the Michigan Institution and graduate of the American School, as an instructor in the deaf department. He also began skillfully raising money from Congress. He received appropriations for salary in 1858, and in 1860 he had the funds of the Washington Manual Labor School and Male Orphan Asylum transferred to the Columbia Institution. In the meantime, Kendall was persuaded in 1859 to construct at his own expense a large brick building. In 1862, Congress appropriated $9,000 for additional buildings, and the state of Maryland agreed to send its deaf children to the Columbia Institution for their education. Gallaudet was now ready for the next step.[31]

His 1862 annual report of the Columbia Institution recommended to Congress that a college be established for deaf students. In 1864 Congress agreed and passed legislation, which was signed by President Abraham Lincoln in April, allowing the Columbia Institution to grant collegiate degrees. The Columbia Institution then was divided into two departments, with the collegiate department named the National Deaf-Mute College, a name it held until renamed Gallaudet College in honor of Thomas Hopkins Gallaudet and then renamed again, in 1986 by an act of Congress, Gallaudet University.[32] The college's official opening occurred in June of 1864. Among the speakers were Laurent Clerc and John Carlin, two deaf men whose efforts to elevate the educational status of deaf Americans had contributed to the college's success.[33]

And it was successful. In 1893 Gallaudet looked back over twenty-nine years of effort with satisfaction. He wrote that in less than three decades the college had produced fifty-seven teachers, four ministers, three newspaper editors or publishers, fifteen government civil servants, a nationally known botanist, two architects, a city councilman, a chemist, three individuals who had founded schools for deaf children in the West, two professors in the college, and a lawyer who had been admitted to practice before the Supreme Court of the United States.[34] The college's first degree, however, was an honorary master of arts, fittingly awarded to John Carlin in 1864 during the inauguration ceremony.

Carlin's commencement address, delivered upon acceptance of the college's first diploma, expressed the pride surely felt by many deaf Americans: "I thank God for this privilege of witnessing the consummation of my wishes, the establishment of a college of deaf-mutes." The opening of the National Deaf-Mute College, he told the watching dignitaries, "is a bright epoch in deaf-mute history. The birth of this infant college will bring joy to the mute community."[35] To make this birth as smooth as possible, Gallaudet moved quickly to assemble the students, faculty, and curriculum upon which any college depends.

George T. Dougherty was an example of a successful Gallaudet student. Graduated with a Bachelor of Science degree, he went on to study chemistry at Washington University in St. Louis and received a Master of Science degree from Gallaudet College in 1885. Dougherty served as vice-president of the NAD and two terms as president of Chicago's Pas-a-Pas deaf club.

By the fall of 1864 Gallaudet had the college ready to open. By the end of its first year it had five collegiate students from four different states and three full-time faculty. Two other persons, William W. Turner, the retired principal of the American School, and James W. Patterson, a former professor at Dartmouth College and then a member of Congress from New Hampshire, were employed as part-time faculty. Patterson, who could not sign, presented a unique problem, but one that Gallaudet solved. Patterson's lectures, Gallaudet wrote, "will be rendered into the sign language by an interpreter. This translation being simultaneous with his uttered words, at the same time not interfering with, or interrupting them."[36] Gallaudet thus instituted a tradition of using interpreters, when necessary, to assist the college's educational endeavors.

Gallaudet also instituted the preparatory class. His 1865 annual report explained that this class was necessary because of three factors. First, he wanted the course of study at the National Deaf-Mute College to be "the full equivalent of that adopted in similar schools of learning for the hearing and speaking."[37] Second, he did not want to admit unprepared students, but he knew that most schools for deaf pupils did not have a "high class" that concentrated on fitting students for further academic work. Gallaudet realized that residential institutions concentrated their resources on occupational training rather than academic achievement, and, in his words, "no uniform standard of graduation prevails." Thus most deaf graduates of state institutions, no matter how bright they might be, would simply not have the background necessary to begin college-level study. Finally, he wished to open the college to all "worthy and intelligent graduates of any institution," not just to those from the few schools with college preparatory programs. The college, therefore, would undertake to offer capable students the remedial preparation needed to fit themselves for the rigors of collegiate study. "These pupils," Gallaudet wrote, "will be instructed wholly by members of the College Faculty, and our object will be to prepare them as rapidly as practicable for admission to the Freshman class."[38]

Such admission was not easily gained, however, for Gallaudet was serious about making the National Deaf-Mute College a respectable institution of higher learning. Applicants for admission had to be recommended by the principals of the schools from which they graduated. Gallaudet personally reviewed and decided upon on all applications during the nineteenth century. After acceptance, each

By the 1870s, a dapper Edward Miner Gallaudet had become a skilled advocate for deaf Americans and a remarkably successful college president, regularly winning Congressional support for Gallaudet College.

student was given a battery of examinations. The fields covered were arithmetic, algebra to quadratic equations, English grammar, ancient and modern history, geography, physiology, philosophy, and "the principles of Latin Construction," especially Latin etymology and syntax.[39]

Students who gained admission were expected to pay $150 annually for their room and board. Gallaudet realized, however, that many would not have the means to pay this sum, and from the beginning the college attempted to find a way to support all deaf pupils who had the desire and the ability, but not the money, to pursue college study.

The initiation of the preparatory class and the college's generous financial aid signified Gallaudet's commitment to make higher education available to a broad segment of the American deaf community. The college he founded would neither restrict itself to those students who had attended the few residential schools with the resources to offer college preparatory courses nor admit only those students from wealthy families who could afford the expenses of college room, board, and tuition. The primary criteria for acceptance would be ability and desire, not previous schooling or financial means.

In one respect, though, the National Deaf-Mute College was not so egalitarian. After initially accepting four female students into the

Agatha Tiegel of Pennsylvania was one of the first female graduates of Gallaudet College. She became a teacher at the Minnesota School for the Deaf in 1893, and there met her future husband, Olof Hanson.

preparatory class, for the next twenty-two years Gallaudet refused to accept any more. Finally, in 1886 he acceded to the demands of young deaf women, and they too were offered admission, though at first only as an experiment.[40] With bright and energetic men and women receiving college educations, before the end of the nineteenth century deaf Americans were in an unusually strong position, capable of shaping and developing a deaf community stronger and more resilient than that of any other country.

8

Organizing

Congregated in residential schools and urban centers, deaf Americans began in the nineteenth century to create a bewildering array of organizations. First was the New England Gallaudet Association of Deaf-Mutes, formally begun in 1854; dozens more followed over the next 125 years. Among the more prominent were the National Association of the Deaf, state associations of the deaf, alumni associations of the residential schools and of Gallaudet College, the National Fraternal Society of the Deaf, the American Athletic Association of the Deaf, National Congress of the Jewish Deaf, and the American Professional Society of the Deaf. Additionally, deaf people in most large American cities founded literary, religious, and athletic associations exclusively for themselves. Deaf social "clubs" opened in even small or medium-sized cities, and deaf individuals gathered together in organizations related to careers and hobbies.[1]

The ubiquitousness of American deaf organizations is striking, but of more significance—because of its uniqueness—is the fact that these have been groups *of* rather than *for* deaf people. In the United States deaf people created their own associations, funded them, and controlled them. In this respect the American deaf experience contrasts dramatically with the experience of deaf people in other nations, where historically most organizations were established for deaf people by hearing people. The paternalism of foreign deaf organizations often meant that, however well-meaning their administrators, their primary focus was on the expectations and needs of hearing people.

American deaf organizations, on the other hand, most often grew directly from the self-perceived needs of their deaf members.

*By the early twentieth century, many large cities in the United States had
one or more deaf social organizations such as the Brooklyn Guild of the
Deaf, photographed here in 1910.*

Foremost among these was association with individuals who shared
similar communication methods, cultural values, and experiences.
Other needs were more concrete. The National Fraternal Society of
the Deaf, for instance, is primarily an insurance company. A group
of deaf men formally chartered it in 1907 when life insurance firms
controlled by hearing people believed that deaf clients—who would
not respond to auditory warning devices, such as train whistles or
automobile horns—presented too much risk and refused to insure
them.[2]

Often organizations created for one purpose eventually served
many functions. The National Association of the Deaf (NAD), the
oldest and most powerful nationwide deaf group in the world, is one
example. From humble beginnings at a meeting in Cincinnati, Ohio,
in 1880, it grew to become a lobbying and consumer rights organization with permanent offices, full-time paid executives, a multimillion
dollar budget, and widespread influence on national and international issues of importance to deaf people. Nevertheless, the NAD

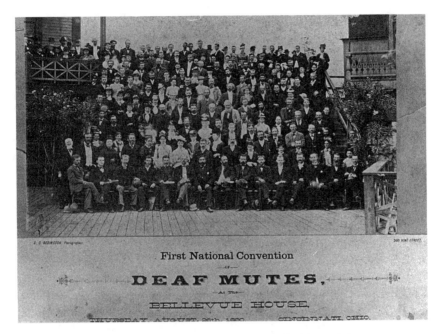

First National Convention
—OF—
DEAF MUTES,
—At The—
BELLEVUE HOUSE.
THURSDAY, AUGUST 25th 1880.   CINCINNATI, OHIO.

The first meeting of the organization that became the National Association of the Deaf.

began and has remained for over one hundred years an organization deaf persons manage for themselves. Today it continues to serve its members by drawing them together, through periodicals and the sponsorship of various activities, to associate with each other and to recognize and act upon their shared interests.[3]

THE NEW ENGLAND GALLAUDET ASSOCIATION

The New England Gallaudet Association of Deaf-Mutes, named for Thomas Hopkins Gallaudet, established precedents that would be followed by other, similar groups. It began informally from meetings of alumni of the American School in 1853. In 1854 the alumni, "desirous of forming a society in order to promote the intellectual, social, moral, temporal and spiritual welfare of our mute community," wrote and approved the first constitution of an organization of, by, and for deaf Americans.[4]

That constitution stated membership principles that were both inclusive and exclusive. Both males and females could join. Men had to pay a fee of one dollar per year or ten dollars for a lifetime; women, whose incomes (when they had them) were smaller than men's, could join for fifty cents annually or ten dollars for life. Most language in the constitution referred to the members as "mutes," that is, as persons who could not, or did not, speak. Yet section two of the article dealing with membership stated explicitly that individuals who were "only deaf or have never been in any institution for deaf mutes" also were eligible to join the organization if they paid the requisite fees. The only people excluded from membership were hearing persons, though they could subscribe to the organization's periodical by paying a subscription charge.[5]

The constitution's distinction between "mutes" and people who were "only deaf" seems anachronistic today, but it marked an important distinction in the middle of the nineteenth century. At that time, in the United States, most deaf persons did not receive speech training in residential schools. Persons who became profoundly deaf when infants or very young children were presumed to be incapable of producing articulate speech. To these individuals, lack of speech was their major identifying characteristic and they unashamedly called themselves "mutes." They saw nothing derogatory in this term and used it proudly. Laurent Clerc, for example, never spoke and yet was considered a well-educated and widely respected person, both among other deaf people and among hearing persons. To say that some individuals were "only deaf" was to indicate that they lost their hearing in adolescence or adulthood and therefore retained speech that could be readily understood by hearing people. Within the deaf community, and among teachers and ministers who worked with deaf people, persons who could not hear but who could speak intelligibly were called "semi-mutes."

The New England Gallaudet Association, however, did not wish to emphasize these distinctions. Realizing the organization's novelty and consequent weakness, the founders sought to include all persons who could not hear. The fact that a person had once heard, or had never attended a school for deaf people, did not exclude him or her. The association realized that it was to the advantage of all deaf people to act in unison, not to be divided by the distinctions that hearing people were apt to apply. The fact of deafness, alone, was a sufficient characteristic to define a person's identity within the deaf community in the middle of the nineteenth century. Persons born deaf, those who lost their hearing in their youth, "semi-mutes," and even people called "semi-deaf"—today's "hard-of-hearing"—were all welcome to the deaf community.

Hearing people, although excluded from membership and not permitted to vote in meetings, were permitted to take part in the Gallaudet Association's activities. At the first general convention of the association, held in 1857 in Concord, New Hampshire, several hearing people were present. The major "oration" at that convention was delivered in sign language by Laurent Clerc, and Thomas Gallaudet, an Episcopal minister and the son of Thomas Hopkins Gallaudet, served as interpreter for the hearing people who attended.[6] Later meetings followed a similar pattern, with a hearing person fluent in sign language given the responsibility of translating into spoken English the convention's deliberations.

A major topic of discussion at the first few meetings of the Gallaudet Association was a publication. The constitution stipulated that the organization would produce a "Society Organ," meaning a "newspaper or periodical." Some deaf people did read the American Annals of the Deaf, but, as pointed out at the 1859 meeting of the Board of Managers of the Gallaudet Association, the Annals was "better suited to the use and benefit of the teachers" than to most deaf individuals.[7] Gallaudet Association members, like those of future exclusively deaf organizations, wanted to publish and to read a periodical that would reflect their specific concerns. Whereas the Annals was primarily interested in deaf education, deaf adults had much broader interests than could be served by a professional journal.

The result was the Gallaudet Guide and Deaf-Mute's Companion. A monthly begun in January of 1860, the Deaf-Mute's Companion was edited by a deaf man who had some newspaper experience, William Martin Chamberlain, and was published in Boston.[8] While it only survived for five years, the Deaf-Mute's Companion marked the first of numerous attempts by deaf people to found, publish, and market periodicals exclusively for themselves. Like the organization that sponsored it, the Deaf-Mute's Companion was a recognition of a growing deaf self-awareness and a realization that deaf Americans were different from hearing Americans, that they had interests that could best be met through their own efforts.

STATE ORGANIZATIONS

The New England Gallaudet Association of Deaf-Mutes was regional, drawing people from Connecticut, Massachusetts, Rhode Island, New Hampshire, Vermont, and Maine.[9] Deaf citizens of these states shared for many years the same residential school, the American School in Hartford, Connecticut, and thus it was natural that they should join together in an organization that crossed state boundaries. More commonly, though, the difficulties and expense of travel to distant meetings, the lack of social ties with deaf people from other states, and the tendency of residential schools to serve almost exclusively the residents of one state meant that successful organizations were local or at most statewide. Among the earliest of the statewide groups was the Empire State Association of Deaf-Mutes.

Henry Rider, for eight years the president of the Empire State Association, in 1877 discussed the reasons why deaf people congregated in exclusively deaf assemblies. Describing a deeply felt social need, he said that the biennial conventions of the state associations were "to us, what the oases of the Great Desert are to famishing travelers." Rider lived in Malone, New York, a small city in the far northeastern section of the state, near the Canadian border, and he described the lives of deaf people in smaller towns as "tedious monotony" that was relieved by meetings of their state associations. His discussion stressed the sense of isolation and loneliness that made Flournoy's deaf commonwealth scheme popular with some people, like the Indiana farmer P. F. Confer. Rider also believed deaf people's partial isolation from hearing people, because of communication differences, caused the latter to have a lack of sympathy for "deaf-mutes as a class." Among themselves meeting in convention, though, deaf people could air their grievances and discuss with sympathetic comrades the discriminations and problems they faced.

Even if deaf people had not felt isolated and lonely, Rider believed, they would have come together anyway. He thought that deaf people were a distinct group, a cultural entity within what he called the "common community." As such they had, in his words, a "natural and predominating affinity for those of [their] own kind."

Rider readily admitted that deaf peoples' natural inclinations toward association were encouraged by the state residential school system. Indeed, he emphasized the importance of the school experience. The usual affection of boarding school pupils for each other,

Rider said, was fostered during school days and afterward permeated the lives of deaf people. In language growing ever stronger, Rider continued that the residential experience "engenders in our hearts the longing desire and almost irresistible impulse to meet with each other; and even though it be brief, to enjoy for a short season the society of our boon companions."[10]

Ironically, later in the nineteenth century hearing people who believed that deaf persons were becoming too clannish, and intermarrying too frequently, would attack the residential school system for doing exactly what Rider said it did.[11]

THE NATIONAL ASSOCIATION OF THE DEAF

The National Association of the Deaf is the oldest nationwide organization founded by disabled people. For the first eighty-four years of its existence, only deaf people were admitted to membership, and, despite the acceptance of hearing people as members, deaf people have remained firmly in control of the association.[12] The first meeting of what became the NAD occurred in Cincinnati, Ohio, in August of 1880, at a perilous time for deaf people.[13]

By 1880 deaf people faced two related challenges. One was the transformation of the United States from a rural agricultural society to an urbanized industrial nation. This national metamorphosis raised the possibility that deaf people would not be prepared, vocationally or socially, for the world that was being created. The other challenge was a determined assault on the traditional methods of teaching deaf children. Alexander Graham Bell, many parents of deaf children, and a growing corpus of hearing teachers were beginning to attack sign language and the residential schools, claiming that they had pernicious effects on deaf people and American society. In short, the conditions known to the first generation of America's deaf community were disappearing.

At least intuitively aware of these facts, and recognizing that deaf persons were being dispersed over wider and wider areas, several deaf people conceived the idea of a national convention of deaf-mutes. Held for three days, attended by deaf representatives from twenty-two states, and at first chaired by the venerable (seventy-year-old) Edmund Booth, this convention discussed issues of importance to all deaf Americans and established the National Association of the Deaf.[14]

The convention's purpose and promise were articulated clearly by Theodore A. Froehlich, one of two representatives of the Manhattan Literary Association of Deaf-Mutes of New York. Froehlich grasped the essential point that deaf people, as they had become educated and had begun to interact with each other in social and educational matters, were becoming a class—an identifiable group apart from the rest of American society. "So far as I understand the object of this Convention," he wrote, "it is to bring the deaf-mutes of the different sections of the United States in close contact and to deliberate on the needs of deaf-mutes as a class by themselves."[15]

Not only were deaf people characterizing themselves as a class when they established the NAD, they also were insisting on their need to control their own destinies. Froehlich wrote that deaf persons must "attain the ability to intelligently administer [their] affairs," and he believed that mutual association provided the best means to this end. His statement in support of the NAD also argued that one objective should be to make all deaf people "capable to enter upon all vocations in life." This goal too, Froehlich believed, "can best be gained by fostering and forming associations."[16]

The establishment of the NAD marked a turning inward by the deaf community in the face of stress and change. Deaf people looked to themselves for the leadership and the strength they would need to confront an environment that appeared hostile to their best interests. Their leaders—men such as Booth of Iowa, Edwin Hodgson of New York, and Robert McGregor of Ohio—understood that power depended on organization and unity. The number of educated deaf persons had increased steadily with the spread of residential institutions and the opening of the National Deaf-Mute College, but without a national body to unite them in common purpose, they would be thinly scattered and isolated over the vast reaches of the United States. The NAD held out the promise of becoming such a national body, although, in reality, deaf people more often identified with their local organizations that could serve their needs on a daily basis.

THE DEAF-MUTES' UNION LEAGUE

The NAD, the New England Gallaudet Association, and the numerous state deaf associations all were significant to the long-term stability and cohesiveness of the American deaf community, but in larger cities local organizations were more popular. They provided for deaf people the sense of belonging and comradeship that ethnic ghettos provided for the immigrants pouring into the United States in the late nineteenth century. Deaf persons in America's cities often were separated from their families both physically and linguistically. Isolated from their hearing neighbors and coworkers, they sought each other out for social interaction, to find potential spouses, to engage in athletic and intellectual pursuits, and to unite in common philanthropic or religious endeavors. One well-documented example of a late-nineteenth-century deaf social club was the Deaf-Mutes' Union League of New York, founded in 1886.

The Union League seems, superficially, to be a most unusual deaf club. All its members were graduates of the Institution for the Improved Instruction of Deaf-Mutes, commonly called the Lexington Avenue School, for its location in New York City. The Lexington Avenue School was a purely oral school; that is, it was a school that did not use sign language or fingerspelling in its classrooms. The first such school established in the United States, it was founded by an Austrian immigrant, Bernard Engelsmann, who previously had taught in a Jewish school in Vienna before moving to the United States in 1864. On March 1, 1867, the school opened, and in 1869 a group of parents and benefactors incorporated it as a private philanthropic organization. One year later, the New York State Legislature agreed to support it on the same basis as the New York Institution for the Deaf, the venerable signing school headed by Isaac Lewis Peet.[17]

Unlike the majority of deaf Americans, the graduates of the Lexington Avenue School were themselves mostly oralists, deaf persons who abjured signs and fingerspelling in favor of speech and speechreading. The club they organized reflected their unusual outlook and confined its membership to alumni of this oldest American oral school. In every other respect, however, the Union League was a typical deaf club.

It began very modestly on January 3, 1886. Four Lexington Avenue School graduates, all men (for this was, and would remain, a male club), met in the parlor of one of the graduate's homes and decided to establish an organization of Lexington Avenue School alumni. A week later they wrote a constitution and by-laws and elected themselves all officers. Within about one year several more deaf men had joined. The original parlor in which the four young men had met now was too small for the larger group. They then moved to 1915

Madison Avenue, where they met in the billiard room in the home of David Bachrach, wealthy father of Arthur Bachrach, one of the new members. In new surroundings and with more members, the group began to develop a sense of purpose, for which the old constitution and by-laws proved inadequate; hence they were replaced by new ones that established committees to carry out the club's functions. On April 17, 1887, the group officially christened itself the Deaf-Mutes' Union League.

The Union League quickly developed activities to enrich the intellectual and social lives of its members. A Committee on Debates and Lectures arranged readings and discussions for the regular meetings that were held twice a month. In the fall of 1888 the organization held its first ball, a formal affair that raised two hundred dollars for the Gallaudet Home for Aged and Infirm Deaf-Mutes at Wappinger's Falls, New York. An annual banquet was inaugurated on January 3, 1889, to commemorate the organization's founding.[18] In the same year the group helped to raise money for the statue of Thomas Hopkins Gallaudet and Alice Cogswell that now graces the front of the Gallaudet University campus and sent several representatives to the National Association of the Deaf meeting in Washington, where the statue was dedicated on June 26.[19] By 1900 the club had the financial strength to send one of its members, Francis Nuboer, to attend the International Congress of the Deaf in Paris. Upon Nuboer's return, the Union League organized a banquet at fashionable Martinelli's on Fifth Avenue.

As the Union League grew in numbers and activities, it searched for new quarters. From the Bachrach's billiard room, it moved to the playroom of the Lexington Avenue School, then to the Central Opera House on Sixty-seventh Street. Here the group put in furniture and a pool table to make a more congenial location for young men to congregate informally and socialize. When the opera house was torn down, the Union League—ever more financially secure—was able to rent at $500 per year an entire floor of a building on Broadway, where the members again installed a pool table and other accoutrements of a private club. For two years the Union League lost some of its participants to a splinter group, called the Lexington Athletic Club. In two years this group disbanded, and its members rejoined the Union League.

By the early twentieth century, the Deaf-Mutes' Union League was a solid organization. It had nearly $2,000 in the bank, a regular meeting place, a full calendar of social endeavors, a long membership list, and even honorary members, such as Edwin A. Hodgson, second president of the NAD and editor of the *Deaf-Mutes Journal*, and the deaf French sculptor, Ferdinand Hamar.[20] Like other local deaf organizations, the Union League survived because it satisfied deaf people's needs. Its activities brought deaf people together to mingle with each other and to work toward common interests. Lectures, debates, pool games, banquets, balls, and charitable fund raising all enriched deaf lives. The need for this kind of mutual activity among deaf people, no matter what their communication method, was starkly and ironically demonstrated by the Union League.

The irony was that the league's members were all orally educated. The great virtue of oral education, according to its proponents then and now, is that it supposedly prepares deaf people for social intercourse with hearing persons. Armed with the ability to articulate clearly and to read speech from the lips, graduates of oral schools such as the Lexington Avenue School were supposed to venture out into hearing society and function as though they were hearing themselves. They were supposed to choose their friends and spouses from among the larger society of hearing people; they were not supposed to be inclined to seek the society of other deaf persons. Yet the Union League, whose members were all graduates of the Lexington Avenue School and were all proud of their oral training, banded together deaf oralists just as the more numerous local organizations of signing deaf people congregated them. Close ties of affection and mutual self-interest among deaf Americans, no matter how they were educated and despite the best efforts of some hearing individuals and organizations, seemed inevitable as the twentieth century began.

9

Cultural Connections

In 1849 the North Carolina Institution for the Deaf and the Blind launched *The Deaf Mute*, a periodical that unwittingly became the pioneer of an important deaf tradition. After the Civil War other institutions followed North Carolina's example—Ohio initiated its journal in 1868; Illinois in 1870; Kentucky in 1873; Virginia, Michigan, and Nebraska in 1874; and so on.[1] By the late nineteenth century, residential school periodicals were ubiquitous. From the *Texas Mute Ranger* to the *Silent Hoosier*, nearly fifty school papers were published by deaf institutions.[2] Known collectively as the "Little Paper Family," or simply the "Little Papers," eventually they assumed a significance out of proportion to their size.

The Little Papers began for very practical reasons. Written, edited, and printed on campus by the residential schools' students and instructors, they provided vocational training for deaf pupils. In the years of linotype machines, printing became the most important single occupation for deaf men. It was a career that offered substantial financial rewards, prestige, employability, and access to a wide deaf and hearing readership. Most of the deaf community's leaders in the late nineteenth and early twentieth centuries were printers at some point in their lives. The Little Papers, however, provided another significant function for the nascent deaf community in the late nineteenth century: they served as the cultural connections that established and maintained group cohesion.

THE IMPORTANCE OF THE WRITTEN WORD

Although the most salient characteristic of deaf people is their use of nonwritten gestural language, by the end of the nineteenth century periodicals written in English intimately linked the disparate members of the American deaf community. Like all Americans, deaf people moved about in search of employment and better social opportunities; yet, even more than hearing individuals, those who were deaf wished to retain ties with their school friends and with others who shared their cultural attributes. One means to do so was through frequent conventions of the state, regional, and national organizations mentioned in the previous chapter. These were, however, inadequate to maintain consistent exchanges of information. For this purpose, newspapers and periodicals written by and expressly for deaf people were the answer.

The publications were generally of two types: either the independent newspapers, such as Hodgson's *Deaf Mutes' Journal* in New York, O. H. Regensburg's *National Exponent* in Chicago, and Philo Packard's *National Deaf Mute Gazette* in Boston, or the Little Papers. In the long run, the latter were more successful. They could depend upon their residential school sponsors to provide the necessary funds to keep them solvent, even if their subscriptions were inadequate to cover

The second president of the National Association of the Deaf, Edwin A. Hodgson edited the excellent Deaf-Mutes' Journal *and taught printing at the New York School for the Deaf.*

Oscar H. Regensburg, *who graduated from Gallaudet College in 1890, managed the* National Exponent, *an independent deaf newspaper published between 1894 and 1896.*

expenses, and they could tap a ready supply of eager (and unpaid) student workers.

Residential schools stated from the outset that their Little Papers would serve multiple purposes. One of these always was to teach printing, but the others were broader, such as to inform patrons of the school's activities, to assist students in literary studies, to teach reading, and to keep the general public abreast of the school's programs and goals. The most important function in terms of the deaf community's viability, however, was to exchange news about deaf individuals and groups and to provide cultural guidelines for deaf people.[3]

CULTURAL GUIDANCE

The educated deaf leaders of the late nineteenth and early twentieth centuries were intensely concerned about the public behavior of their deaf peers. They wanted to make sure that deaf people did not do anything that would cause hearing society to look down on them, fearing that the actions of one deaf individual would reflect negatively on deaf people as a class. Behavior that might be overlooked in a hearing person, or attributed to the weakness of that one person, might be construed by a prejudiced hearing public as a characteristic of all people who could not hear. Deaf people were in this respect, as in so many others, like ethnic minorities. Thus, the public drunkenness of one Irishman—to use a common stereotype from the period—was said to indicate that all people from Ireland drank too much. The illiteracy, laziness, rudeness, or immorality of one deaf person could be used to label the entire class of deaf people as illiterate, lazy, rude, or immoral.

The Little Paper editors and writers therefore filled their columns with advice about correct behavior. In 1891 the Arkansas *Optic*, for example, began one issue with a long article about the evils of the lottery, followed by short pieces with such titles as "Advice to Young Men" and "How to Keep Your Friends."[4] The most famous of the Little Papers, the New Jersey School for the Deaf's *Silent Worker*, in December of 1888 ran a long essay titled "Beer and Tobacco. Our Opinion of These Very Bad Habits" that suggested that a deaf individual's life was difficult enough without adding vice. "We think that for our boys [presumably deaf girls were immune from this kind of temptation], it is very much the best plan to avoid alcohol, in every form," the article reasoned, "whether beer, wine or whiskey, and to have nothing to do with tobacco, snuff or cigars." To drive home the importance of this guidance, the writer went on to argue, "a deaf-mute has to run the race of life under a heavy handicap, and he can not afford to load himself with any extra weight."

Since one of the primary purposes of deaf education was to fit deaf people for jobs, the relationship between proper behavior and success in careers was emphasized in the Little Papers. *The Silent Worker*'s lecture against alcohol and tobacco made this link clear. The essay argued realistically that "many [hearing] people do not want to hire a deaf person." The deaf person, therefore, had to be even more careful of behavior than his or her hearing counterpart. "You will never find it a recommendation to any employer that you drink or smoke," the paper admonished its deaf readers; "other things being equal, the non-smoker and the non-drinker has a better chance of securing employment than the man who indulges these habits."[5]

GOSSIP

The familiar connotations of gossip are negative, but in fact gossip plays an important role in maintaining group standards of behavior and in focusing attention on individuals, giving news a personal dimension. The Little Papers recognized these functions of gossip and included it in their pages.

Most Little Papers carried polite, never malicious, gossip in a feature called "The Exchange" or "Exchanges." These were excerpts from other Little Papers that the editors thought would be of interest to local readers. They kept deaf individuals aware of what was happening in different parts of the United States, and in particular, in the various residential schools. News of events such as marriages, births, deaths, and promotions of deaf people were reprinted, as was news about the curriculum and policies of the schools themselves.[6] Exchange articles also served as self-criticism, for Little Paper editors freely, but again politely, commented on each other's work.

The Silent Worker of May 26, 1892, carried the following items that demonstrate the many functions of the exchanges.

> The Silent Press announces its intention of moving its plant to Chicago.
>
> Dr. Greenberger's school [The Institution for the Improved Instruction of Deaf Mutes] had a narrow escape from being destroyed by fire on the morning of May 14th. The fire was discovered by Supervisor Nuboer [a deaf man] and the engineer, who extinguished it with a few buckets of water. It is not known how the fire originated.
>
> Waco, Tex., has a deaf-mute barber by the name of Tom Williams.
>
> We have been favored with a copy of the "Fanwood Quad Club Journal" published at the printing office of the New York Institution February last. It speaks well for the quality of work which this well-known office is capable of turning out.
>
> The St. Louis Deaf-Mute Club will hold a picnic at Upper Creve Coeur Lake, on June 16.
>
> The deaf press says that there is a deaf-mute by the name of George W. Patton, residing in Illinois, who is studying for the ministry, he being a member of the Methodist Episcopal Church. It is understood that he is to preach to the mutes as often as he can in Terra Haute, Ind.
>
> The Silent World [Pennsylvania Institution for the Deaf] announces the glad news that Mr. Van Allen [an instructor] who has been seriously ill, has passed the crisis, and is expected to fully recover.
>
> F. McGray, a well educated deaf-mute, keeps a well stocked grocery store down in Searcy, Ark.[7]

Although at first glance such items may seem trivial, they were not so to a community whose members were widely scattered, discriminated against, and easily isolated. The exchanges kept deaf individuals aware of the existence and activities of others who shared their cultural characteristics. They quietly indicated that deaf people had many career options, that they could become barbers or grocers or ministers or competent newspaper editors. This message needed to be delivered to the hearing people who read the Little Papers and to those who were deaf. Sometimes, though, the Little Papers addressed the problems of the deaf community more directly.

CONTROVERSY

The Little Papers' treatment of controversial topics was inevitably problematic. Deaf editors often wanted to speak out on issues of importance to the deaf community, but their positions were not secure. Although many schools for deaf pupils were founded by deaf individuals, by the late nineteenth century almost all school superintendents were hearing persons, and the boards of control or trustees of both private and state-supported schools were entirely composed of persons who could hear. The deaf editor who published opinions that conflicted with those of his superintendent risked losing his job. The pages of the *Nebraska Journal* in 1911 provide an example of the awkward position faced by deaf Little Papers editors.

In 1911 the Nebraska School for the Deaf became the object of national attention when the state enacted a law mandating that oral methods—speech and speechreading, rather than sign language and fingerspelling— be used for all instruction in the school. The president of the Nebraska Association of the Deaf was J. W. Sowell, the head teacher at the Nebraska School and the editor of the school's Little Paper. Before the oral law passed the legislature, Sowell adamantly criticized it in the *Nebraska Journal*. He wrote that the proposed law threatened the "welfare of the deaf child, from an educational, spiritual, and even self-supporting point of view . . . as never before was it threatened." When the bill became law, Sowell realized that he had taken too extreme a position, and he began to retreat. The intent of the law, he now editorialized, was merely "to secure a little more stress upon oral teaching; [the governor] did not propose to see the manual method of instruction done away with."[8] Sowell's position weakened still further when a new superintendent was named. This person was Frank Booth, ironically the hearing son of Edmund Booth, one of the founders of the NAD.

*James W. Sowell, a deaf teacher and editor
of the* Nebraska Journal, *had to change
this Little Paper's editorial position when
the Nebraska School for the Deaf got a new
superintendent, Frank W. Booth, who was
an ardent oralist.*

Booth had been general secretary of the American Association
to Promote the Teaching of Speech to the Deaf (AAPTSD), and he
was well known for his extreme hostility to sign language. He enthusiastically took the superintendency of the Nebraska School with the
intention of completely banishing sign language and fingerspelling
from its classrooms. When he made this clear to the school's staff, the
deaf teachers realized that their jobs were not secure. To argue with
Booth, they assumed, would be professional suicide. In consequence,
Sowell, once a leader of the movement to oppose the exclusive use of
speech and speechreading, now refused to take any stand against it.
Henceforth, the editorials in the *Nebraska Journal* either said nothing
about oralism or they praised it.[9]

Little Papers editors often treated controversial issues circum-
spectly. Near the end of the nineteenth century two of the most vex-
ing and worrisome problems for deaf people were attacks on sign language use and deaf intermarriage. *The Silent Worker*, for example, ran
a series of articles on both of these issues in 1890. The opinions of
Alexander Graham Bell, who opposed both (and with whom very few
deaf people agreed), as well as those of Philip Gillett, superintendent of the Illinois School for the Deaf, and of Edward Miner Gallaudet were printed.[10] Gallaudet was received most favorably.

A long article in *The Silent Worker* approvingly summarized
points Gallaudet had made in a *Science* magazine article. In it, Gallaudet argued that most deaf people should marry whomever they

wished, but he cautioned against deaf people with deaf parents and other deaf relatives from marrying "on general principles," though he did not believe that a single rule could be applied to all individuals. Gallaudet saved his strongest arguments for the sign language question. Here he supported the position of most deaf people, that sign language offered the surest means of education for most persons who were deaf, though he did not deny that the ability to speak and read speech from the lips were worthwhile attributes. In short, he supported the so-called combined system of deaf education, that is, a system that allowed the use of signs or speech as best fitted the needs of particular students.[11]

Whatever the response of Little Papers to controversies facing the deaf community, these periodicals became a source of unity for deaf Americans. Through the exchange of ideas and information, deaf people kept abreast of each other's actions. They saw that they were not alone in facing the problems of living in a hearing world. The papers helped to establish and maintain cultural norms, emphasizing that deaf people were different from their hearing contemporaries and that they had unique needs they alone could satisfy.

10

The Assault on Sign Language

Language is the most important attribute of many minority groups, and it has been so for deaf Americans. American Sign Language is not poor English; it is unique. It not only differs from English in its syntax and vocabulary, its visual form is so strange to hearing people that for decades it was not recognized as a language. The significance of sign language to deaf people is obvious from their history. With very few exceptions, the associations, conventions, clubs, and marriages of deaf Americans uniformly reflected the importance of sharing this communication method. They found it rapid, facile, and precise, unlike speech or speechreading. Despite the importance of signs to deaf adults, however, in the late nineteenth and early twentieth centuries the language brought to America by Laurent Clerc and modified by the students and teachers of the American School began to lose its dominant status in schools for deaf children. By 1920 American schools reported that 80 percent of their deaf students were educated without signs or fingerspelling.[1]

After enjoying widespread support in the United States throughout the first half of the nineteenth century, in the latter years of that century sign language went on the defensive. Alexander Graham Bell, hearing parents of deaf children, misinformed politicians, and many hearing teachers and their professional associations attacked signs. They believed that sign language was pernicious and that it should be banished from schools. Bell argued that sign communication made deaf Americans different from their hearing peers; he insisted that it encouraged the growth of a narrow deaf culture and that it perpetuated negative genetic traits.[2] Hearing parents objected to sign language because they believed its use prevented their children from practicing speech and thus being "normal." Politicians thought that instruction by means of sign language made deaf education needlessly expensive. Hearing teachers and their professional associations argued that signs interfered with the socialization of deaf children, as the use of languages other than English supposedly interrupted the socialization of immigrant children. Such charges against sign language were not limited to the United States.

SIGN LANGUAGE IN EUROPEAN SCHOOLS

Some European schools for deaf children almost never used sign language in their instruction of deaf children. Foremost among these were German schools that followed the oralist pattern established by an eighteenth-century teacher, Samuel Heinicke.[3] In the nineteenth century oralism (that is, the method of conducting all instruction in speech and requiring students to learn only through speechreading) was usually called the German method. The first American school to adopt this method, the New York Institution for the Improved Instruction of Deaf Mutes (1867), was founded in New York City by a German-speaking Austrian immigrant; and, in heavily German Milwaukee, Wisconsin, German speakers founded an oral deaf school as early as 1878.[4]

Other countries, especially France, were at one time noted for their nearly exclusive dependence on sign language and fingerspelling in the instruction of deaf students. In the eighteenth century an immigrant from Spain and Portugal named Jacob Rodrigues Pereire had taught a few wealthy French students with oral methods, but France was known for the techniques pioneered by the Abbé Charles Michel de l'Épée. The founder of the Paris Institution for the Deaf, Épée established a sign language tradition in France. Unlike Pereire or his contemporary, Samuel Heinicke, Épée believed that teaching speech to deaf people was purely mechanical. Practicing it in school, he thought, interfered with the time students needed to study the usual academic subjects.[5] The views of Épée and his followers, one of whom founded the first school for deaf students in Italy, prevailed in France and in Italy far into the nineteenth century; hence, instruction in sign language became known as the French method.

Schools in the Scandinavian countries and in England, Spain, and the Netherlands did not uniformly embrace either the French or German methods of instruction during most of the nineteenth century.[6] In the late 1870s, though, this began to change.

THE MILAN CONGRESS

An 1878 meeting in Paris, grandiosely called the International Congress for the Improvement of the Condition of Deaf-Mutes, declared that "preference should be given to the method of articulation and lip-reading," rather than to sign language and fingerspelling, in the education of deaf children. Although attended by only twenty-seven people, this meeting drew public attention to a growing late nineteenth-century controversy between proponents of sign language and the advocates of speech and speechreading in deaf education. To resolve the debate between educators who favored sign language and those who believed in speech alone, the Paris congress called for a larger meeting two years later. Joseph Marius Magnat, a former oral teacher from Switzerland, received support from wealthy descendants of Pereire to organize the larger meeting—which would be called the Milan Congress.[7]

In the meantime, oralists in France and Italy were preparing the groundwork for the congress. French oralists prevailed on the government to issue a report stating that sign language lacked grammar and that its use prevented deaf people from understanding French. The minister of the interior then ordered all schools supported by the French government to use oral French, not signs or fingerspelling, and the head of the Paris Institution, who supported sign language, was fired and replaced by an otologist, a medical doctor, who had no sympathy for or understanding of signs.[8]

In Italy, Catholic clerics completely dominated the field of deaf education and carried the banner of oralism toward the Milan convention. Abbé Balestra, head of a school for deaf children at Como, and Father Tommasso Pendola, of the Siena School, began in the 1870s to try to convert other schools to oralism. Pendola, once an advocate of sign language, became a zealot for speech and speechreading. He launched a periodical to spread his new faith in oralism and organized the first Italian Congress of Educators of the Deaf to develop support for his attempts to have sign language teaching eliminated from Italy's schools for deaf children. Together, the French and

Thomas Gallaudet, the eldest son of Thomas Hopkins Gallaudet and Sophia Fowler Gallaudet, was an Episcopal priest who established St. Ann's Church for the Deaf in New York City. He was one of the American representatives to the Milan Congress.

Italian oral teachers planned the upcoming international conference at Milan.[9]

The Milan convention drew 164 participants from various European countries and the United States, but the majority—a combined total of 143—were from Italy and France. Hearing delegates numbered 163; one delegate, James Denison, principal of Kendall School in Washington, D.C., was deaf. The American delegation included five

A graduate of the American School for the Deaf, James Denison became principal of the Kendall School in 1869 and remained its head until 1909. He was the only deaf delegate to the Milan Congress in 1880.

people—Denison, Edward Miner Gallaudet, his brother Thomas Gallaudet, Isaac Lewis Peet, and Charles A. Stoddard, a member of the board of directors of the New York Institution. Vastly outnumbered by the Italians and the French, the Americans were nearly alone in their belief that sign language should be used as a method of instruction in the education of deaf children.

The issue of methods, Edward Miner Gallaudet wrote, "engrossed the time of the Convention to the exclusion of almost everything else."[10] Twelve speakers gave their opinions on this issue: nine spoke against signs; three (the Gallaudet brothers and Richard Elliot, an English teacher) argued for them. Abbé Guilio Tarra, the conference president, used a two-day-long presidential address to advocate speech and denigrate sign language. He also proposed to the convention delegates the following motion:

> The Convention, considering the incontestable superiority of speech over signs, (1) for restoring deaf-mutes to social life, and (2) for giving them greater facility of language, declares that the method of articulation should have the preference over that of signs in the instruction and education of the deaf and dumb.[11]

It passed nearly unanimously. Only six people voted against it—the five Americans and Richard Elliot.

The Milan Congress thus seemed to give international approval to the idea that deaf children should be forced to communicate without sign language. The influential London *Times* stated as much in an editorial. It wrote that the Milan Congress proved that among teachers of deaf pupils there was "virtual unanimity of preference for oral teaching."[12] The *Times* reported that demonstrations given at the convention had shown how successful oral teaching was. Italian deaf students, the article said, "were addressed just as if they were not deaf, in spoken language, and they one and all answered in spoken language."[13]

The *Times's* enthusiastic report on what was seen and heard at the Milan convention was characteristic of popular press reports on oralism. Finding a way to teach deaf people, who were commonly referred to as "deaf-mutes," to talk seemed a miracle of modern pedagogy. It made sensational headlines and reassured people that society was indeed progressing, that it was learning to overcome the problems of disabilities from which some of its members suffered. Reporters, and their gullible readers, seldom knew deaf people or knew enough about deafness to evaluate what really was happening when a deaf person spoke clearly or seemed able to read lips without hesitation. By contrast, three Milan participants who had spent their professional lives in deaf education—Edward Miner Gallaudet, Richard Elliot, and James Denison—reported that the Italian students who demonstrated speechreading skills began their answers to questions before the person speaking the questions had finished asking them. All three concluded, therefore, that the questions and answers had been rehearsed beforehand.[14]

The *Times* reporters, and most other individuals who sensationalized reports about oral teaching, did not understand the diversity among deaf people. By all indications the Italian children who spoke at the Milan Congress had clear voices, easily understood. Yet this does not mean that oral teaching methods were responsible for developing this useful skill. The *Times* failed to inquire whether these children were born deaf or whether they had in fact learned to speak before losing their hearing. If the latter were true, then it was not teaching methods but rather the fact of previous hearing ability that accounted for the students' speech. Similarly, those who claimed wonders for oral methods did not discuss the degree of hearing loss of their "deaf" students; yet it is a commonplace that a person with some hearing in the speech frequencies will learn speech much more readily than one who is profoundly deaf.

The same kind of sensationalism and lack of familiarity with the varying characteristics of deaf individuals that marked the *Times* report on the Milan Congress also was prevalent as the debate over teaching methods heated up in the United States.

EARLY CHALLENGES TO SIGN LANGUAGE

The American School, under the leadership of Thomas Hopkins Gallaudet and Laurent Clerc, had established in the United States a firm tradition of sign language use in schools for deaf children. Gallaudet, and perhaps Clerc as well, believed that the primary purpose of schools was to impart religious truth to deaf pupils and to familiarize them with the knowledge all persons needed to function in an increasingly complex world. For these purposes, instruction by means of sign language seemed ideal. The language was quick, sure, and readily mastered by persons unfamiliar with any written or spoken language.

In the 1840s, however, Horace Mann, an educational reformer from Boston, challenged sign language and called for the use of oral methods in American schools for deaf students. After a visit to Germany, where he saw oral methods in practice, Mann insisted that such methods should be used in the United States. George E. Day of the New York Institution and Lewis Weld of the American School disagreed. They too visited Germany in 1844, as did Isaac Lewis Peet in 1851, and all agreed that Mann's claims for the effectiveness of oral methods were exaggerated; thus, Mann was ignored.[15]

Shortly after the Civil War, Mann's arguments received new attention as oralism began to make inroads. Teaching by means of speech and speechreading alone began to gain adherents in private schools, where parents had more influence than they did in the state residential institutions, which the professional educators controlled. The first such oral school opened in New York City in 1867. At about the same time a group of wealthy New Englanders, who were primarily concerned that their deaf children should learn to speak, founded

The second oral school established in the United States, and one of the few remaining in existence, is the Clarke School for the Deaf in Northampton, Massachusetts, established in 1867.

the Clarke Institution for Deaf Mutes in Northampton, Massachusetts. Clarke was an oral school that attempted to prohibit the use of signs or fingerspelling in all aspects of its students' lives.[16] These events did not go unnoticed by those who believed in the value of sign language.

In 1868 Edward Miner Gallaudet, fresh from his own visit to European schools, warned the heads of American schools for deaf children that they would have to begin teaching speech in their schools. For too long, he argued, Americans had relied totally on manual methods. Gallaudet said that the time had come for American teachers and administrators to combine the best features of both oral teaching and sign language teaching. He also urged teachers to use fingerspelling rather than signs wherever possible to help deaf students learn English.[17] Yet the one individual most responsible for advocating speech and speechreading as a panacea for the difficulties of deaf people had not yet even arrived in the Western Hemisphere when Gallaudet delivered his warning.

At this meeting, Edward Miner Gallaudet (front row and center) warned administrators of signing schools that they would need to give more attention to teaching speech and speechreading in their institutions.

ALEXANDER GRAHAM BELL

Alexander Graham Bell emigrated from England to Canada in 1870. To hearing people Bell is best known for his invention of the first successful telephone, but to deaf people in the late nineteenth and early twentieth centuries he was best known as their strongest adversary in the controversy over sign language. George Veditz, two-time president of the NAD and a brilliant deaf leader, described Bell as "the most to be feared enemy of the American deaf."[18] Ironically, Bell's mother was hard-of-hearing. With an ear tube (a primitive hearing aid) she usually could follow one-to-one conversations and even play the piano, but her hearing was so weak that Bell grew up using the two-handed English manual alphabet to communicate with her in situations when she could not hear conversation.[19] Bell's wife could not hear at all.

Bell first came to the United States in April of 1871 to teach articulation by means of a system his father invented. Called "Visible Speech," this method was supposed to enable deaf or hearing people to understand and to produce the precise mouth shapes and movements necessary to create perfectly all the sounds of all languages. In the United States Bell first employed his father's system at the Boston School for Deaf Mutes, a public oral school (later renamed the Horace Mann School), and he instructed private pupils as well. At this early stage in his experience Bell did not believe that speechreading was effective, and he did not initially use it with his deaf students. To his father he wrote, "in my descriptions [of Visible Speech] I use either signs or the blackboard, or the manual alphabet."[20] He was confident, however, that Visible Speech instruction held the key to intelligible speech for all deaf people, and he staged an exhibition on November 28, 1871 to prove it.

His exhibition attracted a large audience, including, Bell said, "all the influential Educationalists of Boston."[21] Bell gave them an impressive show. His father, grandfather, and uncle were accomplished dramatists, used to performing readings and lectures on a stage in front of audiences, and Bell put his experience with them to good effect. He first explained the supposed scientific principles of Visible Speech, and then three of his students "performed." All three were young women, which surely made Bell's presentation especially attractive to the overwhelmingly male crowd, and each did something different. Alice Jennings, who had normal hearing and speech until

Alexander Graham Bell, the inventor of the telephone, led the attempt to have all deaf Americans taught speech. He also was concerned that the growth of an American deaf community would be disadvantageous to the United States, although his mother was hard of hearing and his wife was deaf.

struck with scarlet fever at age eight, recited clearly and distinctly, thereby presumably showing that articulate speech was possible for a profoundly deaf person.[22] The second student, Isabel Flagg, sang and told a funny story about thrushes and starlings with some words altered, Bell wrote to his parents, so "that she might pronounce them well."[23] Flagg, however, was not deaf. She heard fairly well with an eartube, and she could carry on conversation without any mechanical or visual assistance when spoken to slowly.[24]

Bell was not a charlatan, however. Although he shrewdly exhibited a hard-of-hearing pupil and one who had been deafened long after learning speech, for these were the deaf people who spoke most normally, he thought that Visible Speech would work to teach articulation to people born profoundly deaf. To demonstrate this point he exhibited Theresa Dudley. His manner of doing so showed that he possessed a remarkable flair for appealing to his audience.

Dudley was the daughter of a wealthy Northampton, Massachusetts, family. Profoundly deaf since birth, she had been educated at the American School in Hartford and later at the Clarke School, which her father helped to found. When she was seventeen years old, in September of 1871, her parents sent her to Boston to work with Bell, for they were not satisfied with the speech she had acquired at Clarke. They continued to hope that a method could be found to improve it, and Bell promised to do so with Visible Speech. Communicating with her primarily by writing, Bell tried to develop her ability to produce any sound that he indicated with Visible Speech symbols.[25] The results of this effort he put on stage at his November 28 exhibition.

Bell exploited his audience's interest in the exotic and their appreciation of the familiar. First, he had Dudley pronounce individual words from a variety of foreign languages. He then asked people in the audience to utter words from any language. Next, he wrote down their composite sounds in Visible Speech symbols, and Dudley—from seeing the symbols Bell wrote for her—would produce the foreign word, or at least a sound resembling it. He also had her make strange sounds for the audience. These, he said, were Zulu "clicks," thus demonstrating that Visible Speech could be used to represent the sounds of any language, not just English or the more common tongues of western Europe.[26]

By this point Bell had the audience's attention and interest. Next he got their sympathy and admiration by having Dudley not only say words but actually recite sentences from Visible Speech symbols. The selection she read, and which had been practiced thoroughly beforehand, was the Lord's Prayer. Though, by Bell's own admission, her speech was not fluent and distinct, it did not matter.[27] Everyone in the audience would have been able to follow this most common of prayers no matter how poor Dudley's speech skills.

Bell was not a religious person; he was a skeptic who did not attend church and did not believe in the value of prayer. Nevertheless, he chose the Lord's Prayer for Dudley's recitation because it was already known to his audience and, therefore, would appear to be spoken more clearly than would an unfamiliar text, and because it would appeal to the listeners' sympathies. With this exhibition, Bell demonstrated a flair for attracting attention and winning converts to his beliefs. With few exceptions, his deaf opponents lacked such skill.

Bell's exhibition was a success. It helped launch his career in the field of deaf education. He gained introduction to influential people in Boston, and his father's Visible Speech was hailed as a new and scientific technique to teach deaf people to talk. Both the American School and the Clarke School invited Bell to try his method with their students and to teach it to their instructors. In the spring of 1872 he did so, spending two months at each school.

An insatiably curious and energetic man, Bell used his time at the American School well. He read all he could in the school's library about the history of deaf education. He also learned enough American Sign Language to use it with some ease. Bell found his time at Clarke somewhat disturbing, for he was shocked that the teachers refused to use fingerspelling with their students.[28] From his experience with his mother, Bell at first believed that deaf people could not learn to read speech from the lips well enough to substitute speechreading for the manual alphabet. He later modified this opinion.

Back in Boston after his time at Northampton and Hartford, Bell became acquainted with a few deaf people who could speechread easily. Most important of these was a young pupil named Mabel Gardiner Hubbard. The daughter of a wealthy Boston attorney and businessman, Gardiner Greene Hubbard, Mabel had become deaf at age five from scarlet fever. She and a few other private students of his, especially Jeannie Lippit, daughter of the governor of Rhode Island, and Josey Annon, could speechread much better than deaf people Bell had known before, and they all spoke well enough to be understood by most hearing people.[29]

Bell eventually fell in love with and married Mabel Hubbard, but more importantly his experience with her convinced him that speechreading was a practical alternative for deaf people. For the rest of his life, then, Bell dedicated himself to the cause of speech and speechreading. He believed that deaf people could, by using oral methods, become sufficiently like hearing persons to function without sign language and to participate fully in all the activities of hearing society. He used the enormous prestige and great wealth he earned from his invention of the telephone to advocate this position for the remaining fifty years of his life.

DAY SCHOOLS

The assault on sign language took two paths in the late nineteenth century, one of which was the advocacy of day schools for deaf children. Beginning in the 1880s and reaching a peak in the 1890s, Bell and a few other American oralists promoted day schools as a solution to the problems that they saw in the American system of instructing deaf children. Day schools did not have residential facilities. In theory, though not always in practice, all day students lived at home with their parents and only attended the school during the day, just as hearing children did at their local schools. Day schools thus had to be numerous, scattered throughout populated areas, just as hearing schools were. The low incidence of deafness made this idea impractical earlier in the nineteenth century, for few cities had enough deaf children to justify the establishment of a school for them alone. Residential institutions overcame this problem by attracting students from a wide geographic area and providing them with room and board away from home.

Bell and some other oralists began in the 1880s to challenge this rationale for the residential institution. By that time the United States was a rapidly urbanizing nation, with more and more people, hearing and deaf, crowded together in urban centers. Thus, day school proponents argued that a class of local deaf children could be formed in even medium-sized cities. Bell suggested that this class of deaf children—this day school—would not have to stand alone but could be attached to the local hearing, public school. Younger deaf children would have their own teacher for most subjects, but they would be integrated with the hearing children for recess, sports, drawing, vocational training, and other activities that presumably did not require the student to understand exactly what the teacher was saying. By this means, deaf children theoretically would become accustomed to communicating with hearing people by means of their voices and speechreading. Away from deaf adults and from teachers trained to use sign language, deaf children would not develop the pernicious signing habit, and they would feel more comfortable in hearing society than in the deaf community. When they became old enough, those with sufficient academic skills would go on to attend regular, public high schools.

The day school experiment began in Wisconsin. The Wisconsin Phonological Institute, a philanthropic society dedicated to oral training of deaf children, twice tried to convince the Wisconsin state government to fund day schools in every Wisconsin city that could put together a class of five deaf pupils and hire a teacher. When the Phonological Institute failed in its two attempts, its energetic president, Robert C. Spencer, invited Bell to visit Wisconsin.[30]

Spencer reasoned that Bell, by the 1880s world famous, energetic, and wealthy, could use his influence and prestige to convince the state legislature and the governor to support day schools. Bell accepted Spencer's invitation and visited Madison, the state capital, in the summer of 1884 and again in the winter of 1885. During his first visit he addressed a meeting of the National Education Association, arguing in favor of the day school principle.[31] In his second visit he spoke to the education committees of the state legislature and prepared for them a long paper explaining the value of day schools for deaf children.[32] Bell's efforts bore fruit; in 1885 Wisconsin became the first state to allocate money to support day schools in any community that wished to have them.[33]

As expected, day schools proliferated in Wisconsin's cities and larger towns during the 1880s and 1890s, and they used no sign language. Most of their teachers were trained in the Wisconsin Phonological Institute's normal school. They were all young hearing women, and all were committed to the idea that deaf people should be integrated with their hearing peers and should not form communities or use sign language.[34]

The day school idea was attractive to state legislators. Its advocates promoted day schools as inexpensive alternatives to residential schools, since the state did not have to pay for room and board or the relatively high salaries of the male hearing administrators who headed the residential schools; it only had to pay the low salaries of female teachers. In 1900, for example, Robert Spencer claimed that the cost of educating a deaf student at the Wisconsin residential school was $316 per year, whereas it was only $150 per year in Wisconsin's day schools.[35] Day schools also seemed to have the advantage of keeping young children at home with their parents, where nearly everyone believed that they belonged. Students who attended residential schools often did not see their parents for months at a time. Both parents and legislators worried about the supposed ill effects of the lack of parental discipline and affection resulting from this separation.

It is not surprising, therefore, that the day school idea caught on elsewhere. By the 1890s, day school laws similar to those in Wisconsin had been adopted in California, Illinois, and Ohio, and they were being considered in several other states.[36] Still, oralism would not have succeeded unless it had converted the state residential institutions for deaf students. The administrators and teachers in those schools often were politically powerful and, therefore, influential; furthermore, many people—sometimes including Bell—realized that the residential schools could not be eliminated because small local day schools just could not provide the diversity of courses and the array of resources that most deaf children needed to become fully functioning, taxpaying citizens.

CONVERTING THE INSTITUTIONS

Bell's efforts in behalf of speech for deaf people initially met skepticism among many residential school teachers and among most deaf people themselves. Though many teachers, like Edward Miner Gallaudet, thought that persons who were hard-of-hearing or who had lost their hearing after learning to speak could develop their voices, they were skeptical about the possibility of speech and speechreading for the majority of deaf people, especially those born deaf. Bell at first made little progress in his attempts to convince these people to give up their signs and fingerspelling and use purely oral methods. To strengthen the oralist position among teachers, Bell and other oralists organized.

American oralists realized that the main professional organizations of teachers of deaf students, the Convention of American Instructors of the Deaf (CAID) and the Conference of American Principals and Superintendents of Schools for the Deaf, were dominated by Edward Miner Gallaudet in the late nineteenth century. Thus Bell and his supporters founded two rival groups, Department 16 of the National Education Association (NEA) and the AAPTSD.

Bell's connection with the NEA began in 1884. At the urging of Robert Spencer, the president of the NEA invited Bell and other experts on deaf education to join the NEA's general meeting in July to discuss with NEA members the relation of deaf education to the public schools.[37] Following this meeting, informal "round tables for teachers of the deaf" were held at subsequent NEA conferences until 1897. Then Bell and other oralists persuaded the NEA to establish a permanent department, Department 16, for "teachers of the deaf, blind and feeble-minded."[38]

Through the NEA, oralists were able to develop widely based support for their antisigning, pro–day schools position. NEA members were teachers and administrators in regular, hearing schools. Their natural sympathies favored day schools, with which they were familiar, rather than boarding schools, and they could empathize with the stated goals of oralists, whether they worked in day schools or in residential institutions.

Oralists sought to develop the social skills of deaf students. Their primary goal was not education in the traditional sense of imparting facts and analytical skills to their pupils, but to make deaf children as similar to hearing children as possible, to fit them into American society. In the same way, teachers in regular schools began, in the 1890s, to believe that their main function was to socialize their pupils.[39] Carroll G. Pearse, president of the NEA in 1911, stated that the purpose of all education, whether of deaf or hearing children, was "to so train young people that they may take their places and be useful in society."[40] Or, as one historian has summarized the attitude of hearing teachers, "the child was now conceived not as a mind to be developed but as a citizen to be trained by the schools."[41] Oralists agreed.

Oralists also used their public relations skills to convince NEA members that speech and speechreading should supplant signs in the education of all deaf children. This was most dramatically demonstrated at the 1897 meeting in Milwaukee that established Department 16. Oral day schools in Wisconsin and Illinois sent numerous teachers and, more importantly, what Bell described as a "continual supply of pupils and classes" to demonstrate the success of oral methods. The effect of cute young deaf children's speaking and understanding the speech of their hearing teachers in demonstration classes must have been profound. Most NEA members surely were unfamiliar with the speaking ability of deaf people. Bell himself was amazed at the failure of sign proponents to bring their students and exhibit their achievements, and he recognized that this was a tactical error. He wrote to his wife that

> the general failure of institutions and sign schools to send pupils brought the oral system prominently forward. All the schools of the country were invited to participate and the preponderance of oral pupils was due to the failure of sign-schools to take advantage of the opportunity to impress public-school teachers.[42]

Although oralists successfully enlisted the NEA in their struggle against sign language, their primary organization for advocating the benefits of speech and speechreading was the American Association to Promote the Teaching of Speech to the Deaf (AAPTSD), today's Alexander Graham Bell Association for the Deaf. Founded in 1890 at a meeting of the CAID, the AAPTSD became the vanguard of the American pure oralism movement.[43] Bell contributed $25,000—an enormous sum in 1890—toward the organization's endowment and periodically donated even more money for its operating expenses. The AAPTSD organized annual meetings, like its rival CAID, and it established in 1899 a semiprofessional journal called the *Association Review* (today the *Volta Review*) to counter the *American Annals of the Deaf*, which was still controlled by people favorable to sign language.[44] Unlike Department 16 of the NEA, the AAPTSD appealed to oralist teachers and administrators in large residential schools that traditionally used oral methods, such as the Clarke school and the New York Institution for the Improved Instruction of Deaf Mutes, and to those in the traditionally sign language schools who were becoming interested in oralism.

Under Bell's astute leadership the AAPTSD tried to reach a larger public than just teachers of deaf students. The *Association Review* sought to carry articles of a general interest as well as those more specifically focused on deaf education.[45] The AAPTSD and Bell's private research laboratory, the Volta Bureau, willingly supplied information to parents of deaf children and to state legislators and journalists interested in issues related to deafness. In this way, oralists hoped to build broad public support for their policies and beliefs, and they were generally successful.

INSTITUTIONAL CHANGES

The efforts of Bell and his colleagues showed steady progress through the 1880s and 1890s and into the twentieth century, as teachers and school administrators changed their attitudes toward the relative value of sign language and speech. In 1882, for example, only 7.5 percent of the 7,000 pupils in American schools for deaf children were taught orally (that is, without signs or fingerspelling).[46] By 1900 that percentage had increased to 47. The year 1905 marked a watershed— for the first time in American history the majority of deaf students learned without the language bequeathed to them by Clerc and Thomas Hopkins Gallaudet. Speech, speechreading, and writing, rather than sign language and the manual alphabet, were the communication methods used to instruct the majority of deaf pupils in the United States.[47] By 1919, at the peak of oralism's influence, schools reported that nearly 80 percent of deaf students received their instruction and communicated with their teachers without any manual language. Though this figure may have been an exaggeration, for deaf children could not easily be prevented from signing, it was neverthe-

By 1900, most state residential schools taught speech to their pupils, like these in the Maryland School for the Deaf in Frederick. Note the girl using a mirror and a hand on her throat to try to "feel" her speech.

less true that the pendulum had swung radically against the traditional communication method of American schools for deaf students. This change came about both through external pressure on residential institutions and from internal decisions. An example of the latter case was the Pennsylvania Institution for the Deaf.

Founded in 1820, the Pennsylvania school was the third oldest American school for deaf children. After an unsteady beginning, during which the first principal, David Seixas, resigned amid accusations that he had molested a female student, Clerc himself took the principalship and organized the instructional program. On loan from the American School, Clerc established sign language as the method of instruction, and he set the institution on its feet.[48] By the end of the Civil War the Pennsylvania Institution had a fine reputation as one of the top schools for deaf children in the country and one of the fastest growing. In 1870, for the first time, the school decided to experiment with speech teaching.

The Pennsylvania Institution's conversion to pure oralism was slow, paralleling the general movement away from sign language in

DAVID G. SEIXAS.
First Principal of the Institution.

When David G. Seixas, a hearing man, resigned as principal of the Pennsylvania School for the Deaf, Laurent Clerc took over the school's direction and established a signing tradition that continued until the 1890s.

late-nineteenth-century America. Initially, one teacher taught a single articulation class to students who had lost their hearing after acquiring speech (semi-mute) or were hard-of-hearing (semi-deaf). In 1876 an articulation department was established; the person named to head it, Edward Crane, had studied Visible Speech with Bell at Boston University.[49] That experiment proved unsatisfactory, however, and in 1881 the school decided to separate its oral department physically from the manual (signing) department in order to remove most of the oral students from a signing environment.

By 1885 the Pennsylvania Institution was teaching speech and speechreading in three different contexts. At the main building some students received speech lessons for half an hour or forty-five minutes each day and took their other classes with the manual students. Others in the main building took all their instruction in speech but were allowed to mingle with the manual students outside of the classroom in dormitories, at meals, and in other common activities. A third group of oral students was entirely segregated. They attended classes, ate, and slept in a building apart from the main campus where, at least in theory, no signing or fingerspelling occurred.

Slowly the number of manual students taking speech lessons dwindled, and the Pennsylvania Institution divided its students into strict oral and manual departments. Either students received all instruction in speech and speechreading or all in signs and fingerspelling. In 1892 the school moved into magnificent new quarters in the

Philadelphia suburb of Mt. Airy and completed its separation of speakers from signers. The new campus had two complete sets of facilities on its spacious grounds, one for manual students and one for oral pupils. According to the school's principal, A. L. E. Crouter, teachers discovered that those oral students who previously had been allowed to mingle with signers outside of the classroom were definitely inferior in the quality of their speech and speechreading and their overall academic achievement to those who had been segregated from the signers. Crouter thought this comparison proved that "speech methods and sign or manual methods do not and cannot combine to the advantage of pupils instructed under what are known as combined-system methods." In other words, a pure speech environment was necessary for oral methods to achieve their greatest success.[50]

Not all students succeeded in the oral department. Between 1881 and 1899 about 10 percent of the students originally placed in oral classes did not make satisfactory progress and had to be transferred to the manual classes. This raised the obvious question, in Crouter's words, of whether "these failures [were] owing to the method of instruction pursued, or were they rather the result of inferior mental powers on the part of the pupils themselves?" When only a small percentage of the "oral failures" achieved "even average success under manual methods," Crouter concluded "that it was not the method, but the mental condition of the pupils that was at fault."[51]

A leader in A. G. Bell's American Association to Promote the Teaching of Speech to the Deaf, A. L. E. Crouter converted the Pennsylvania School for the Deaf from an institution that stressed signs to a leader in teaching by means of speech and speechreading.

The Pennsylvania Institution, then, went ahead and converted nearly the whole school to the pure oral system. By 1910, when Pennsylvania was the largest residential school for deaf students in the world, 532 pupils were in the oral department where no sign communication was permitted, and only 71 "oral failures" received instruction through signs and the manual alphabet.[52]

The Pennsylvania Institution rejected sign language by choice. Although a law of 1893 required that all new students be taught under oral methods unless they demonstrated themselves incapable of learning without signs, the school already had committed itself to education without sign language. Both the Board of Directors and Crouter, who was a member of the executive committee of the AAP-TSD, believed in the value of speech and speechreading, and they thought that the use of sign language interfered with deaf students' desire and ability to acquire oral skills. Other schools, however, did not give up signs willingly. Opposition to sign language often developed outside of the school and forced some institutions, against the wishes of their teachers and administrators, to stop using sign language and convert to speech and speechreading.

The most important external influence on the schools was parents, and hearing parents of deaf children were especially responsive to the arguments of oralists. Parents wished their offspring to be "normal," to be just like them; oralism seemed to hold out that possibility. If only their deaf children could learn to speak and to read lips, parents often believed, then they would fit into the family and would remain a part of the culture and community the parents understood. On the other hand, if their deaf children grew up signing, they might not be able to communicate with other members of the family; they would most likely marry another deaf person; and they would join a community—the deaf community—from which their parents were excluded. Whatever the objective truth of these ideas, they were widely held in the late nineteenth and early twentieth century. The AAPTSD, and Bell personally, made every effort to convince parents of their validity.

The Wisconsin Phonological Institute, Bell, and the AAPTSD encouraged parents to take an active role in their deaf children's education by organizing themselves into associations to lobby for oral methods. One successful effort took place in Nebraska.

In 1911 four parents convinced the state legislature and the governor to enact a law requiring the use of the "oral, aural, and lipreading" method rather than the "deaf alphabet and sign language" in the Nebraska School for the Deaf.[53] They accomplished this feat by establishing themselves as the Nebraska Parents' Association for the Promotion of the Teaching of Speech to the Deaf and by using resources the AAPTSD provided. Bell's organization sent copies of the *Association Review* for each member of the Nebraska legislature. Officials in the AAPTSD, at the request of the Nebraska Parents' Association, also wrote letters in support of oral education to key members of the Nebraska legislature and to the governor.[54]

The superintendent of the Nebraska School and many teachers, especially those who were deaf, opposed the bill. As a result, the parents' association pressured the governor to name a new superintendent, one who was firmly committed to oralism. The governor yielded to their pressure, fired the old superintendent, and hired Frank W. Booth, who had been recommended by the parents' association.[55]

Though Booth had deaf parents, he was a committed oralist. He began his career in deaf education at the Pennsylvania Institution, which he helped to convert to oralism. He then went to work for Bell. In 1910 he was editor of the *Association Review*, executive director of the AAPTSD, and the superintendent of Bell's Volta Bureau. In early 1911, for reasons unrelated to events in Nebraska, Booth was fired from his position with the AAPTSD and the *Association Review*. Thus, he welcomed the job offer from Nebraska and quickly took up his new job.[56] He banished sign language from the school and established a separate manual department that used fingerspelling only for students who were, in the words of the 1911 law, "incapacitated by mental defects" from using speech and speechreading. By 1930, 80 percent of Nebraska's students received all their education orally, and sign language no longer existed on the Omaha campus.[57]

Beginning in the late nineteenth century oralists challenged the legitimacy of American Sign Language, the very core of the deaf community. In this endeavor they were led by one of the United States' most famous individuals, a man whose invention, the telephone, symbolized the modern age of science and the potential for new kinds of communication. Yet the deaf community did not collapse or acquiesce to this affront to its language. Despite the efforts of Bell, the Phonological Institute, the AAPTSD, innumerable parent organizations, and state legislatures, the American deaf community fought back and ultimately persevered, unlike many of its European counterparts. American Sign Language never disappeared entirely from America's deaf schools, and it certainly did not lose its strength within the deaf community.

11

The Struggle to Save Signs

Deaf Americans lacked the power to force schools to instruct their pupils by means of sign language. Deaf teachers always were in the minority, even in the oldest residential institutions, and few deaf people became superintendents or principals. Even fewer (if any) deaf individuals sat on school governing boards. Moreover, deaf education in America was decentralized. European national governments or religious groups could dictate pedagogical methods for a whole country, but no single entity had such hegemony over American schools. Nearly every state government, the federal government, private philanthropists, and local school boards all supported educational institutions for American deaf pupils. This very diversity, though it meant that deaf people could never be certain where to concentrate their energies, also meant that opponents of sign language could not achieve their goals easily; and it may help explain the survival of a language that many influential individuals and organizations wanted to destroy. Another factor in the stubborn persistence of American Sign Language, though, was the strength of the American deaf community and the skill of its leaders and spokespersons.

The timing of the oralist onslaught, too, was fortunate for the cause of sign language in the United States. The deaf community already had begun to organize itself; its communication network was in place; and it had a core of educated and forceful individuals to lead it. The NAD originated at a meeting in 1880, just one month before the Milan Congress. School Little Papers were ubiquitous by the late nineteenth century, and their pages carried an endless stream of articles about the fate of sign language and the challenge of oralism.

Stronger articles appeared in the independent deaf press, particularly in the *Deaf Mutes' Journal*, which was achieving its greatest success at the turn of the century. Outstanding individuals such as NAD presidents Robert McGregor, Edwin A. Hodgson, Olof Hanson, Jay C. Howard, and George Veditz provided some of the most vigorous leadership the American deaf community has had. Thus, when the challenge did come, the deaf community was to some extent prepared.

By the early 1870s, when Bell's Visible Speech began to raise hopes for speech and speechreading, most of the arguments against oralism already were well known. Abbé de l'Épée in the eighteenth century and Thomas Hopkins Gallaudet in the early nineteenth had identified many of the obvious weaknesses of speech as an instructional objective and as a pedagogical method for persons who could not hear. Teaching by means of speech alone, they recognized, was maddeningly slow and frustrating for pupil and instructor. Teaching a student to speak was similarly tedious and often bereft of results. Worse, it used valuable time that was necessary to develop the pupils' intellectual abilities and moral sense.[1] Following the apparent success of the Clarke Institution and the New York Institution for the Improved Instruction of Deaf Mutes, some of these old charges against oralism reappeared.

In 1872, for example, Benjamin D. Pettengill of the Pennsylvania Institution questioned the feasibility of oral instruction for the large numbers of students typically enrolled in state-supported residential schools. He made his argument from an examination of both the historical record and from contemporary observation. Discussing the former, he wrote,

> The pioneers in the cause [of deaf education], Ponce, Carrion, Amman, Pereira, and others, certainly brought their pupils to a higher point of attainment than is usually reached in our institutions for the deaf and dumb; not that they employed any peculiar and wonder-working processes in teaching their pupils, but because they had but few pupils to teach, a long time in which to teach them, and taught them language, as I suppose, mainly by practice and usage.[2]

In short, Pettengill argued that it was not an inherent quality of the oral method—although all the teachers he mentioned used primarily speech and speechreading in their teaching—but the fact that their students received intensive and constant instruction that accounted for their success.

Pettengill believed that the Clarke School's ability to teach some of its students to talk and to learn by means of speechreading was due to the same factors. "In the Northhampton [sic] Institution for the Deaf and Dumb," Pettengill commented, "it is to be observed that all the classes are small, and much of the instruction personal and individual." This, rather than method, he insisted, explained why that school attained more success with oral methods than many sign language teachers expected, accustomed as they were to the larger classes of the publicly supported residential institutions.[3] Pettengill's questioning attitude toward the supposed achievements of oral methods was important, but he was even more insightful when he developed justifications for instruction by means of sign language.

Pettengill first dealt directly with the issue of what it means to be deaf and how that affects the educational system for deaf people. He denied that deafness was the terrible disaster that oralists often claimed. Following in the tradition of Épée and the elder Gallaudet, Pettengill wrote that the "chief calamity" and only "serious evil" resulting from congenital deafness (that is, deafness since birth), was "intellectual and moral darkness." It followed, therefore, that the best system of education was that which "most speedily and effectually brings the deaf-mute from darkness to light, most extensively cultivates and improves his intellectual and moral faculties, and the soonest renders him an intelligent, reasonable, and civilized being."[4] Except for the most ardent oralists, few denied that education by means of sign language could accomplish the goals Pettengill set for deaf education. Pettengill dismissed as a mere "inconvenience" deaf people's frequent inability to articulate clearly and to speechread. He was astute enough to recognize, however, that this argument would not have much significance for many parents and teachers who wished, above all, to impart knowledge of the English language to deaf children. He addressed this issue in an 1873 article.

Pettengill challenged the idea, vigorously advocated by oralists, that knowledge and use of sign language interfered with learning English. He wrote that pupils should "write more, and read more, and [finger]spell more; but it does not necessarily follow that they should use signs less than at present." Developing this idea, Pettengill insisted that the obstacle to progress in learning "artificial language" (meaning any spoken language for a deaf person) was not the use of a natural language, but failure to get enough practice with the "artificial" one.

Pettengill used a keen observation to fortify this argument. Anticipating by nearly one hundred years research that would support his contention, Pettengill wrote that he had observed that "the children of deaf-mute parents who have used signs, such as are employed in our institutions, from their infancy, invariably, other things being equal, attain to a correct use of written language sooner than other congenital deaf-mutes who have not had their practice in sign-making."[5] Oddly, this point was ignored for the next one hundred years of arguments over the value of sign language. Indeed, most of the rhetoric used by deaf and hearing people on either side of the oral-manual controversy was uninformed by research.

The deaf proponents of sign language, however, had one weapon hearing oralists did not—personal experience with hearing loss. With very few exceptions, deaf people themselves, from their own experience, believed that sign language was the easiest and most effective communication tool for individuals who could not hear. Though deaf leaders thought that speech and speechreading skills were valuable assets, they doubted whether a significant number of deaf children would ever be able to speak clearly enough to make themselves understood to strangers or would speechread sufficiently well to learn easily in the classroom. Deaf people used their own experience to argue in favor of education that permitted the use of manual language and against day schools that prohibited it.

As the day school movement gained adherents in the mid-1880s, for example, George Wing warned against mixing hearing and deaf children in the same school. Wing, who was hard of hearing, initially had been enrolled in a public school as a child. He found the experience crushing and degrading. He wrote in the *American Annals of the Deaf* that putting a deaf child into such an environment was a "cruel" experiment "and must be barren of good results." Though a fairly good speechreader with an understandable voice, he felt humiliation and discouragement in the public school.[6] By contrast, Wing fit well into the life of a deaf residential school where he could use sign language. He attended and was graduated from the American School for the Deaf and later became a creative and successful teacher in the Illinois and Minnesota Institutions.[7]

Robert P. McGregor, who founded the Cincinnati Day School (which used sign language) and became the first president of the NAD, in 1910 pointedly asked where the oral successes were. If speech and speechreading could create a deaf person who fitted into hearing society, he asked, why could not oralists produce these individuals to testify to their accomplishments? To an NAD convention he said,

> You all know that the "restored to society" deaf person is a standing joke among us. We are always hearing of him, but we have never seen him. Like the Irishman's flea, as soon as we put our finger on him he is sure to be somewhere else, so we have never been able to capture a real simon pure oralistic "restored to society" deaf person and hold him long enough to get him under the microscope and describe him.

Instead of making deaf people fitted for hearing society, McGregor charged, speech and speechreading made them "truly pitiable." "With imperfect speech," McGregor concluded, "they cannot mingle freely with the hearing, and knowing no signs they are equally at sea in a social gathering of the deaf."[8]

Even an occasional advocate of oral methods also wondered why orally taught deaf people did not publicly support speech and speechreading. E. S. Tillinghast, a hearing son of David Tillinghast, had served as superintendent of several western state schools for deaf pupils, and he stated this problem in 1909 at a meeting of the AAPTSD. "It has always seemed to me," Tillinghast told the gathering of oral teachers, "that there is something radically wrong with oralism which cannot turn out deaf graduates who appreciate the value of the methods by which they were instructed." He went on, even more forcefully,

> I thought . . . how thrilling it would be to have a deaf man . . . stand up here and defend the Oral method orally. . . . We do not see such a deaf man here. . . . We have met together to talk about the education of the deaf, and the deaf themselves reject what we are having to say. There must be some very profound reason for this.[9]

The reason was not terribly profound: Most deaf Americans communicated most easily by means of sign language and fingerspelling. They rejected the goals of the AAPTSD and, if they were at all active in deaf advocacy, worked against attempts to eliminate manual communication from deaf schools. One individual who was especially active in attempts to save sign language was Olof Hanson.

Born in Sweden and educated at the Minnesota School for the Deaf and Gallaudet College, from which he graduated in 1886, Hanson was one of the first American deaf architects. He also taught and became an ordained Episcopal minister. In the history of the Ameri-

Olof Hanson was a deaf architect and one of the most powerful leaders of the American deaf community in the early years of the twentieth century.

can deaf community, however, Hanson is best remembered as a tireless advocate. He belonged to several deaf organizations, headed the NAD for three years, wrote voluminously for the deaf press, and helped convince President Theodore Roosevelt to keep the doors of the Civil Service open to deaf workers.[10] Hanson also believed in the value of manual communication for deaf pupils and in 1889 made an unusual suggestion directly to Bell.

At that time Bell was especially concerned about preventing deaf people from marrying each other. This gave him another reason to oppose sign language. Bell argued that using signs prevented deaf individuals from interacting with hearing people and encouraged them to intermarry rather to than find hearing mates. Bell's solution, of course, was that deaf people modify their communication method to meet the preferences of hearing people. Hanson, who apparently had made Bell's acquaintance while a student at Gallaudet, recommended just the opposite. In a letter of February 13, he told Bell that hearing people should change their communication habits to facilitate interaction with deaf persons, and he requested Bell's assistance in achieving this goal.

Hanson's letter was carefully reasoned and polite. It showed the respect that many deaf people, particularly those who knew Bell personally, had for him. Hanson apologized for some of the more extreme criticisms that Bell had received from time to time in the deaf press, assuring him that they did not reflect the opinions of educated deaf people. "I, for one, at least," Hanson told Bell, "beg to express my appreciation of your valuable labors in behalf of our class." Hanson wrote that he agreed with Bell that "the deaf should associate less with one another and more with hearing people," but, he added, "how to bring it about is the difficulty."

Forcing deaf people to attend hearing schools and to give up sign language would not achieve Bell's goal. "No, Dr. Bell," Hanson wrote, "the root [of deaf people's tendency toward exclusive interaction] lies far deeper than that. The deaf are foreigners among a people whose language they can never learn." Hanson argued that speechreading involved merely substituting one form of visual communication that was reliable for another that was less so because "to the deaf, speech is but another mode of signs, and a very poor and indistinct one as compared with any of the other methods." Since most deaf people, according to Hanson, would never be able to learn "the almost universal mode of interchanging thought by speech and hearing," the way to encourage deaf–hearing association (and intermarriage) was "to diffuse a knowledge of the manual alphabet as widely as possible among hearing people."

Hanson believed this could be done by teaching fingerspelling in the public schools. He told Bell that Philip Gillett, the superintendent of the Illinois School, had recommended to the state legislature that training in the manual alphabet be added to the curriculum in

Philip Gillett, for many years superintendent of the Illinois School for the Deaf, was one of the hearing people who argued in favor of the use of sign language and fingerspelling in deaf education.

Illinois. But this idea needed support from a person of Bell's stature. Hanson suggested to Bell that "if you would lend your assistance, either by personally addressing a convention, or in any manner you think practicable, you would do a favor, which, I think, the deaf would much more quickly appreciate than your past services."[11]

Bell never did the "favor." He later explained to a hearing person, who made a similar suggestion, that he believed that it was unrealistic to expect the majority (in other words, hearing people) to learn a special communication method just for the advantage of the deaf minority.[12] Though Hanson failed in this attempt to sway Bell, he continued the struggle to preserve sign language in deaf schools.

THE NEBRASKA CONTEST

Since the United States has no central authority to dictate educational practice throughout the country, the struggle between the deaf community and the oralists took place in a piecemeal fashion. Sometimes the arena was a convention of teachers. More often it was meetings of governing boards or school administrators, places in which deaf people had little influence. Other times it was the pages of deaf periodicals, the Little Papers, and professional journals, but these skirmishes in print were ritualized and had little meaning. The AAP-TSD's *Association Review* was predictably and overwhelmingly in favor of speech and speechreading and opposed to all manual communication, whereas the *American Annals of the Deaf*, until Edward Allen Fay surrendered the editorship in 1920, was open to all opinions but staunchly supported the right of deaf people to use their own language. Yet another arena was state politics, and from 1911 to 1915 the deaf community and American oralists squared off against each other in the state of Nebraska.

The reason was a state law that said, in part,

> All children hereafter admitted to the Nebraska School for the Deaf and all children who have not advanced beyond three years in the course under present methods in said school shall hereafter be taught and trained in said school by the oral, aural [hearing only] and lipreading method to the exclusion of the deaf alphabet and sign language, unless incapacitated by mental defects or malformation of the vocal cords.[13]

In sum, the law required the Nebraska School to follow a particular method for teaching its deaf students, a method that most deaf adults found inadequate and one that precluded deaf instructors. Deaf Americans responded by drawing upon all the resources their community had developed.

The first response came from Hanson. As president of the NAD, he lobbied against the bill to establish the oral law; he wrote to the governor of Nebraska and sent him an "official" NAD statement. The NAD statement contained a number of different arguments against oralism. It claimed, for example, that the law did not recognize the validity or importance of the opinion of its supposed beneficiaries. Hanson claimed that 95 percent of deaf Americans approved of the "Combined System," wherein students who could learn orally were taught speech and speechreading, but others received their instruction manually. The statement said that even those individuals who attended oral schools and thus experienced the method themselves "severely condemn those who would exclude the sign language." The statement also argued that the Nebraska law would not be consistent with usual practice in the United States as "the Combined System is used in the instruction of 80 per cent of the deaf in this country." Oralism, it continued, would be a hardship on deaf students. They would not be able to understand sermons, enjoy lectures, or take part in debates. Finally, the NAD position was that deaf education should be left in the hands of experts, not the state legislature. "It would be just as sensible," Hanson wrote, "for the Legislators to enact that all sick persons must take Osteopathic treatment and no other."[14]

When the oral bill cleared the Nebraska legislature and the governor signed it, deaf people changed tactics. Instead of opposing the new law, they sought to shape its interpretation. At first, they appealed to the new superintendent, Frank Booth. Hodgson wrote an editorial in the *Deaf Mutes' Journal*, optimistically suggesting that Booth was more broad-minded than he had appeared to be when he headed the AAPTSD.[15] Hanson began correspondence with Booth, reiterating the familiar arguments in favor of the combined method and assuring Booth that he could interpret the Nebraska law flexibly, but Booth was not interested. He told Hanson that he would change the Nebraska school to the oral method as quickly and as thoroughly as possible.[16] Various state associations of deaf people (which at the time were independent of the NAD) tried to help their Nebraska peers by influencing the governor. The Minnesota, Mississippi, South Car-

Frank Walworth Booth was the hearing son of deaf parents, Edmund Booth and Mary Ann Walworth Booth. Ironically, he headed the American Association to Promote the Teaching of Speech to the Deaf. Later he became superintendent of the Nebraska School for the Deaf, which he tried to convert to a pure oral school, prohibiting all signing and fingerspelling.

olina, and Kansas Associations for the Deaf, for example, passed resolutions condemning oralism.[17] Booth, though, was equal to the pressure exerted by the deaf community.

In the fall of 1911 he counterpunched and strengthened the oralist position by inviting the head of the NEA, Carroll Pearse, to speak in Omaha. To the Nebraska Teachers' Association, Pearse delivered a blistering attack on sign language and a paean to the virtues of oral teaching. He claimed that students taught by means of signs became "freaks,—dummies," who had no friends and resembled trained dogs, able to perform for their masters but unable to support themselves. By contrast, orally taught deaf people became normal. The deaf children from oral schools, Pearse stated, developed "natural" voices that made them virtually indistinguishable from hearing children. Pearse's address so pleased Booth that the latter published it in Nebraska's little paper, the *Nebraska Journal*, thus notifying the deaf community of his support for Pearse's insulting and radical views.[18]

Yet the deaf community did not give in. Veditz suggested that the NAD raise $5,000 to hire lobbyists and fight the oral law, and a petition drive began.[19] Between 1,500 and 1,700 deaf people signed a letter of protest against strict oralism. Though its fundraising drive was far below Veditz's hope, the NAD did raise $122 in 1912 and in 1913 to support their efforts against Nebraska's law.[20] Hanson attempted to garner political support for deaf people's arguments by sending letters to the three newspapers in Omaha. The letters reiterated the major points in favor of the combined system and added that Gallaudet College's entrance records showed that students educated by this means were more successful than orally trained deaf people in gaining access to the college.[21]

Hanson then increased the political pressure. He wrote letters to the newly elected Nebraska governor, trying to win him to the deaf position, and he used NAD funds to hire Lyman Hunt as a lobbyist.[22] Hunt, a Nebraska School for the Deaf graduate and former teacher, was directed to go to Lincoln, the state capital, and there try to influence legislators in favor of legislation to overturn the 1911 law.[23] At the urging of William Davis, a hearing man from Omaha who worked closely with Hanson, two legislators introduced such a bill in 1913. In support of it, Hanson wrote to all four members of the Senate committee on the "Deaf, Dumb, and Blind," explaining once again why deaf people supported the combined system.[24]

Still, the Nebraska state legislature was not convinced. In 1913 and again in 1915 it defeated bills to overturn or modify the 1911 oral law. After nearly four years of struggle, the Nebraska School for the Deaf became an oral school with a small manual department for "oral failures."[25]

In a sense the American deaf community lost this struggle. The legislative defeats of 1911, 1913, and 1915 seemed to indicate that those hearing people who controlled deaf education listened only to oralists—to the AAPTSD, Bell, organized parents, and the NEA—rather than to deaf individuals or the organizations that represented them.

Yet that is not the whole story. The Nebraska clash also showed that deaf people in America were a community, that they could rally around common interests, and that they could articulate their beliefs. Throughout America, deaf individuals with no personal stake in the Nebraska situation contributed their words, and even a few of their dollars, to assist their peers. The NAD, for the first time, acted in the role of an organized interest group in American politics. It sponsored legislation, paid a lobbyist, and organized a letter-writing campaign. In the 1910s the NAD had not yet achieved the stability and strength it would develop later, but it had laid the groundwork and established the precedent of deaf people working for themselves to further their own interests. Deaf Americans were neither silent nor apathetic as hearing people tried to take away their language.

NG SIGN LANGUAGE FOR POSTERITY

The struggles of the early twentieth century produced two important attempts to document and preserve American Sign Language: Joseph Schuyler Long's *The Sign Language: A Manual of Signs*, and the NAD's film collection.

Long's authorship of a book describing signs is not surprising. A graduate of the Iowa School for the Deaf and Gallaudet College, Long became one of only a handful of deaf people who managed to win and hold administrative positions in deaf education during the early twentieth century. In 1902 he became acting principal of his alma mater and permanent principal in 1908. He also wrote and published poetry and edited periodicals for the deaf community.[26] Like many of his contemporaries in the deaf community, Long worried that sign language might lose its expressive power and uniformity if it was not learned in the form inherited from previous generations. The preface to the second edition of his book, published in 1918, noted that sign language was no longer taught in any school, and "no attempt is made to see that it is learned and used correctly." Thus he hoped that his work would "help to preserve this expressive language, to which the deaf owe so much, in its original purity and beauty, and that it will serve as a standard of comparison in different parts of the country, thereby tending to secure greater uniformity."[27]

J. Schuyler Long hoped to preserve American Sign Language and to keep it uniform by publishing a manual of signs.

First published in 1909, Long's book was a reference, more like a foreign-language dictionary than a modern linguistic text. He used few photographs and employed English word descriptions of hand, face, and body movements to illustrate how particular signs should be formed. Long arranged the book as though English words had exact equivalents in sign, although he stated in the text that sign language was "idiographic" rather than a "word language." Furthermore, Long did not explain the nuances of facial expression, sign sequence, and space utilization that are recognized today as important within the grammatical structure of American Sign Language. Long's work, therefore, was hardly a definitive, or even entirely accurate, depiction of the deaf community's language, but it marked a recognition that its language was worth recording.[28] A more ambitious effort, and one using a more satisfactory medium, was the NAD's project to film the great signing masters of the era.

George Veditz originated this novel idea. Twice elected NAD president, Veditz was an uncompromising foe of oralism and advocate of sign language. Never tactful, the Baltimore native described oralism as "wickedness" and "evil," and he believed that sign language was "the noblest gift God has given to deaf people."[29] During his presidency of the NAD, from 1907 to 1910, Veditz began to raise money to use the new technology of films to record examples of the United States' greatest signers, hearing and deaf. In this way, Veditz believed, American Sign Language could avoid the fate of European sign lan-

One of the brightest and most acerbic leaders of the American deaf community, George W. Veditz initiated an NAD project to preserve American Sign Language on film.

guages, which he thought had degenerated and lost their power after they were pushed out of the schools.

The NAD project lasted from 1910 to 1920. During that decade the NAD captured on film poems, lectures, and stories of the old days rendered in American Sign Language, without voice or lip movement. The signing models included deaf Gallaudet professors John B. Hotchkiss and Amos G. Draper; Edward Miner Gallaudet and Edward Allen Fay, both Gallaudet College administrators; the deaf principal of the New York School for the Deaf at Fanwood, Thomas F. Fox; Robert P. McGregor, first president of the NAD; George T. Dougherty, a deaf chemist; and a deaf Episcopal priest, James H. Cloud. One of the best models and most moving signers was Veditz himself, who delivered an address entitled the "Preservation of Sign Language."[30]

SIGN LANGUAGE LIVES ON

By the 1920s, when the debate over sign language was muted, as it would remain with few exceptions until the 1960s, the deaf community was battered but not beaten. A small core of deaf teachers remained in most state schools, teaching vocational subjects and those students who were considered oral failures. Some victories had been won. In 1905 the Illinois legislature had reversed an earlier decision and withdrawn state support for day schools; in 1912 the New York School for the Deaf, after surveying deaf leaders, had decided not to abandon signs for pure oralism; Long's textbook of signs and the NAD films had recorded sign language for future generations of deaf people; the NAD and other organizations of deaf people were still strong and continued to support the principle of sign-language-based instruction; and Gallaudet College remained a signing school for America's deaf elite.[31] The strength the American deaf community developed in the earlier nineteenth century served it well through the difficult years of the 1890s, early 1900s, and beyond.

12

Marriage

The late nineteenth century confronted deaf Americans with a new threat to their individual happiness and to the maintenance of their community. As persons carrying "defects," their right to marry was questioned. The time was propitious for such a challenge. The manifestations of a deaf community—special churches, schools, newspapers, social clubs—were gaining visibility precisely when the United States entered a period of especially intense racism and speculation about the inheritability of human behavioral and physical characteristics, including hearing loss. Commentators suggested that intractable social problems, such as crime and poverty, resulted from bad genes. The first major American study linking behavioral characteristics and heredity (through several generations of one family, the Jukes) appeared in 1877. The eugenics movement, which sought to improve society by selective human breeding, had begun to gain strength in England and had spread to the United States. Sir Francis Galton, a cousin of Charles Darwin, first used the term "eugenics" in 1883; in the same year Alexander Graham Bell delivered his *Memoir upon the Formation of a Deaf Variety of the Human Race*—a study suggesting that hearing society should take measures to prevent deaf people from marrying each other.[1]

A connection between deafness and heredity had been recognized for decades, perhaps centuries. The Bollings of Virginia, as noted in a previous chapter, had deafness in two generations; Sylvester Gilbert, a hearing man who assisted Mason Cogswell in establishing the American School, fathered five deaf children. In addition to one of Gilbert's daughters, many other pupils at the American School came from families with an apparent tendency toward deafness. Thomas Brown, who entered the school in 1822, had eight deaf relatives, including his father, sister, and aunt; David Beard, who entered in 1829, claimed a deaf brother, deaf sister, and three deaf cousins; Abigail Newcomb, enrolled in 1829, shared deafness with four brothers and two sisters; Rebekah Allen of Hartford, Maine, who entered in 1825, may have held the record. Four brothers and four sisters and eleven of Allen's other relatives were deaf. These and other instances led officials of the American School to conclude that deafness "runs in families."[2]

Families on Martha's Vineyard, a small island off the Massachusetts coast, provided much data for speculation about heredity and deafness in the early nineteenth century. At the American School, and elsewhere, people noted and commented on the fact that deafness seemed to be unusually common among Vineyarders. Modern research shows that during the nineteenth century the incidence of deafness on the Vineyard was in fact phenomenally high compared with other areas of the United States. One child in every 155 born on Martha's Vineyard was deaf. Overall in the United States, only one out of every several thousand children was born deaf.[3] Thus the records of the American School and the families of Martha's Vineyard demonstrated at least a probable link between deafness at birth and heredity. The exact nature of that connection, however, eluded nineteenth-century researchers.

On the Vineyard and elsewhere deafness sometimes ran in families, but it did not seem to be transmitted directly from parents to children. Eighty-five percent of the deaf children on the Vineyard, for instance, had hearing parents.[4] Similarly, all the deaf Bollings were the offspring of hearing individuals. Records of the American School demonstrated that, even among those pupils who had deaf relatives, students rarely had deaf parents; typically the deaf relatives were either siblings or cousins. The confusing nature of the relation between deafness and heredity also appeared in the American School's marriage statistics for the thirty-four years from its founding until 1851. During that period 144 graduates married and produced children. Five of the families thus created had deaf children, yet the overwhelming majority, 139, produced offspring with normal hearing.[5] If deafness was inherited, then, it was not according to an obvious pattern of straight lineal descent. One hypothesis was that consanguinity might explain the seemingly peculiar pattern of deafness in families.

Consanguinity (the marriage of close relatives) was popularly believed to produce harmful results in the children born of such unions. S. M. Bemiss, a physician from Louisville, Kentucky, in the 1850s tried to determine the "proportion of the deaf and dumb, blind, idiotic, and insane . . . who are the descendants of blood intermarriage." Bemiss reported to the American Medical Association in 1858 that he was not entirely successful because of the difficulty of determining whether parents of such children really were related. Nevertheless, he did conclude that more than 10 percent of congenitally deaf children (that is, children born deaf) were "the offspring of kindred parents, or of parents themselves the descendants of blood intermarriage."[6]

Bemiss's study, though, only served to indicate some of the pitfalls that hindered early investigators of the relationship between deafness and heredity. One of these was a logical problem. Merely discovering that 10 percent of congenitally deaf children had parents closely related to each other proved nothing. The fact of consanguinity alone—in the absence of other data—did not mean that consanguinity caused any particular child's deafness. George Darwin, a professor at Cambridge University in England, demonstrated this fact empirically in another nineteenth-century study. Darwin's investigation showed that a small percentage of the deaf children in English schools were, like their American counterparts, the results of unions between first cousins. The percentage of hearing children with parents who were first cousins, however, proved to be the same as the percentage of deaf children. Thus the blood ties of the parents had no explanatory value. If a certain percentage of all people were the result of consanguineous marriages, then some deaf people, naturally, also would have closely related parents.[7]

Another obstacle was that accurate data concerning key issues did not exist and often could not be produced. Family relations, for example, were extremely difficult to determine in the absence of written records covering several generations of marriages and births. Thus, even when parents wanted to cooperate with researchers, their answers were not reliable. On the Vineyard, where all or nearly all deaf people were in fact related, individuals were unaware of extended family relations or ties of blood. A man and woman who married and then had deaf children could believe that they were not related, when in fact they actually shared one or more common ancestors.[8]

It was not possible, either, to determine when a person had become deaf. Aware parents might guess that an infant could not hear, but audition could not be measured in newborns. Yet early researchers on deafness emphasized the significance of the person's age when the hearing loss occurred. They believed that congenital deafness indicated a hereditary cause, whereas they assumed that only disease or accident caused deafness later in life. Both assumptions were (and are) false. People born deaf may have lost their hearing because of prenatal or perinatal (during birth) accident or disease, and the onset of hereditary deafness may occur at any time in a person's life.[9] Nevertheless, these problems, and those much more serious ones caused by ignorance of Mendelian genetics, did not hinder Alexander Graham Bell from spinning theories and delivering warnings about the evils of permitting deaf intermarriage.

A DEAF VARIETY OF THE HUMAN RACE

Bell believed that deafness was a terrible curse to the individual who had it. Perhaps this was a natural prejudice. Bell had grown up in a family whose livelihood depended upon the cultivation and training of the voice, and he had taught young deaf children; thus he had experienced firsthand the serious problems they faced in trying to acquire knowledge through spoken and written language. Bell's bias, moreover, was strengthened by the way he lived. He became in his early thirties a wealthy individual who had little sustained contact with those adult deaf people who were members of the deaf community and who succeeded in finding happiness and personal satisfaction within it. Knowing little of the deaf community, Bell saw it only as a pathological aberration and a threat to the social order that had served him so well.

Bell also believed that deaf persons weakened the society in which they lived. By the 1880s, when he had money and leisure time to pursue whatever interests he wished, Bell grew concerned that the numbers of deaf people in America were increasing. He thought this phenomenon was sapping the strength of his adopted country, and he determined to reverse this trend. Since deafness seemed incurable, Bell focused his efforts on discovering a means of preventing the birth of deaf children. He began by examining the records of several American schools for deaf children, and there he discovered data that he found alarming. These he used to compose a paper entitled *Memoir upon the Formation of a Deaf Variety of the Human Race.*[10] Bell then read his paper to a meeting of the American Academy of Sciences at New Haven, Connecticut, in 1883 and to the Conference of Principals of American Schools for the Deaf in 1884.

The conclusions of Bell's paper were startling. To justify them, he carefully documented three important facts about deaf Americans: first, that there was a "tendency among deaf-mutes to select deaf-mutes as their partners in marriage;" second, that this "tendency" had been increasing during the nineteenth century (that is, more and more deaf people were marrying other deaf people); and third, that this trend would continue into the future unless steps were taken to halt it.[11] These facts were not surprising to most educated deaf Americans or to others familiar with them. What was surprising was Bell's conclusion that "the intermarriage of congenital deaf-mutes . . . should result in the formation of a deaf variety of the human race."[12] And, Bell insisted, "the production of a defective race of human beings would be a great calamity to the world."[13]

Having announced that the world faced a calamity, Bell then theorized how this had developed, how deaf people had come to marry each other. In the past, before deaf persons received education, he said, they seldom married, "and intermarriage (if it existed at all) was so rare as to be practically unknown." During the nineteenth century, however, that had changed. As education became commonplace for deaf people, they began to intermarry. Bell identified seven conditions—most of them related to the educational system—that accounted for the increasing propensity of deaf Americans to marry each other: (1) residential schools; (2) associations and organizations of deaf people; (3) deaf newspapers; including the Little Paper Family; (4) instruction by means of sign language; (5) writing in sign language; (6) erroneous ideas about deaf people; and (7) the desire of deaf people to establish a separate state for themselves.[14]

The fifth and seventh of Bell's conditions were absurd and of no importance—sign language writing was no more than the passing dream of a hearing Irish teacher of deaf students; and the deaf state fantasy had long since collapsed, as Bell knew, because of lack of support from the deaf community.[15] By the sixth condition Bell meant the common idea, which he thought to be erroneous, that deaf people could not be taught to speak and speechread sufficiently well to carry on oral communication easily. The other four conditions were valid, however, and their elimination would have destroyed the American deaf community.

That was exactly Bell's purpose. Bell correctly recognized that sign language, deaf organizations, residential institutions, and the deaf press assisted deaf Americans in creating and perpetuating their own subculture, one in which their concerns and interests—rather than those of hearing persons—predominated. The institutions of the deaf community allowed deaf individuals, most of whom were from hearing families, to find one another, socialize, and marry. Without organizational and cultural links among themselves, deaf Americans would have been isolated individuals, forced to socialize with and marry hearing people or not to socialize and marry at all. Bell believed that isolating deaf people by separating them from each other would force them to think and act like hearing persons and thus (presumably) not produce his dreaded "deaf variety" of humans.

In the Memoir Bell suggested that there were two possible ways to avoid the formation of a "deaf variety" in the United States. One was to develop repressive measures, that is, to enact laws to prohibit all deaf people from marrying each other or at least to proscribe congenitally deaf people from intermarriage. This idea, though, he thought would not work. Indeed, Bell feared that laws against deaf marriage would lead to the evils of sexual promiscuity and illegitimate births. Bell also recognized that it was impossible to prove whether a person was born deaf or became deaf in infancy, and a prohibition of marriage would not necessarily prevent the birth of children to deaf parents. As long as deaf people "of both sexes continue to associate together in adult life," Bell reasoned, "legislative interference with marriage might only promote immorality."[16] Since repressive measures probably could not succeed, Bell recommended instead what he called "preventive measures" to decrease the desire of deaf adults to intermarry.

Bell suggested three "preventive measures": eliminate residential schools, forbid sign language use in the education of deaf pupils, and prohibit deaf adults from being teachers of deaf children. These steps, Bell wrote, would encourage deaf people to use and develop their oral skills, thus making them figuratively less deaf and more easily assimilated into the hearing community.[17] From Bell's standpoint, these "preventive measures" had the advantage of appearing to be educational reforms. They were, therefore, well within the American tradition of using the schools to achieve social goals that could not be reached through coercion.

DEBATING INTERMARRIAGE

Bell's hopes to prevent deaf intermarriage did not seem totally unrealistic in the late nineteenth century. There was precedent for his "preventive measures" in the policies followed by the Perkins Institution for the Blind. Samuel Gridley Howe, who founded Perkins as the Massachusetts Asylum for the Blind and who headed it for forty-four years, refused to allow reunions of its graduates for fear that such contact might encourage blind adults to socialize and marry each other.[18] Howe's successor at Perkins was his son-in-law Michael Anagnos, a person even more strongly committed to prevent blind intermarriage. Though admitting that there were no statistics or published studies of blindness and heredity, Anagnos believed that when individuals who were blind from "organic disorder" had children, they were "invariably sightless." Under his administration, male and female students were separated completely so that they would not develop bonds of affection. Therefore, there was no coeducation, and, he wrote, not "the least inclination on either side for intercommunion or intermarriage." Moreover, Anagnos claimed that from 1833 to 1870 there were in New England only five instances of blind individuals marrying each other; and from 1870—when Perkins began its complete segregation of the sexes—until 1883, no blind couples had taken marriage vows in the New England states.[19]

The possibility of direct legislative interference with deaf marriage could not be dismissed either. Although the eugenics movement did not gain strength in the United States until early in the twentieth century, in 1896 Connecticut led the way in enacting a law against the marriage of people with certain kinds of defects that presumably were inherited. Connecticut was not alone, for several other states followed with their own proscriptions against intermarriage of some people, though not of deaf persons.[20]

Bell's *Memoir* did not lead to a prohibition of deaf marriages in the 1880s, but its proposals did spark debate and instill fear and anger in many deaf individuals. To build support for his ideas, in 1884 Bell printed the *Memoir* and sent copies to members of Congress, the principals of American and Canadian schools for deaf pupils, and innumerable other individuals involved with deaf education in the United States and abroad. Not all were impressed by Bell's data or his conclusions. The principals of state residential institutions questioned whether Bell's concerns were justified. For one thing, they believed that his data were inadequate and suspect. From their personal experience, they believed that deaf couples rarely had deaf children, and that a huge preponderance of their pupils had hearing parents.[21] At the New York Institution, for instance, only 51 of 2,993 pupils enrolled from 1818 to 1883 had even one deaf parent. Of those 51, a mere 22—less than one-tenth of 1 percent of all the school's pupils—had two deaf parents.[22]

Principals raised other issues as well. David Dudley of the Colorado Institution suggested that deaf couples, in his experience, were happier than couples with one hearing and one deaf partner.[23] Isaac Lewis Peet stated perhaps the most pertinent concern, but one that few hearing people ever would understand. He argued that, although deaf couples might occasionally have deaf children, this was not the disaster claimed by Bell and other oralists. "There are many worse calamities than deafness," he wrote, "so much so, that interference with marriage ought to go much farther in other directions."[24]

Deaf people were nearly unanimous in rejecting the idea that they should be prevented from marrying whomever they pleased as long as hearing people had that right.[25] James E. Gallaher, a hard-of-hearing teacher from Chicago, wrote that he hoped that Bell would "not fail to find a cause for children being born deaf and dumb to hearing and speaking parents. It would not suffice to ascribe one's deafness to deaf and dumb parents and allow the other side to pass by."[26] Gallaudet College graduate James L. Smith complained in the American Annals of the Deaf that deaf persons worked among hearing people, that they lived among hearing neighbors, that they engaged in the same amusements as hearing persons, and that this was enough. It was only natural that at least in their domestic relations they should want to be among people with whom they could communicate easily.[27] A deaf Philadelphian, Hiram Phelps Arms, even published a book—The Intermarriage of the Deaf: Its Mental, Moral, and Social Tendencies—attacking the idea that deaf people should choose hearing marriage partners.[28]

Deaf people were most alarmed, however, by an article in the Washington Post on the last day of December 1884. That article stated that Bell had recommended that Congress enact legislation to restrict the rights of deaf people to marry. Although the article was false (Bell never made such a suggestion, for the reasons stated in his *Memoir*), the deaf press picked up the article and circulated it widely.[29] A torrent of indignation followed. Despite Bell's denials, many deaf people continued to suspect that some hearing people wished to prevent deaf marriages.

Bell's correspondence indicates that apparently he found the criticisms he received from deaf people to be amusing, but he was more concerned by the lack of support for his ideas from other hearing persons.[30] To strengthen his arguments concerning the evils of deaf intermarriage, in the late 1880s Bell began a more thorough investigation of the relationship of deafness to genetics. With various research assistants, he scoured the records of Martha's Vineyard and several small communities in New England where there was a high incidence of deafness, and he tried to convince school principals to gather data from their graduates. Over a number of years he expended a great deal of energy and money in an effort to prove the role of heredity in causing deafness. But in the end he failed. Deaf and hearing people produced deaf and hearing children in a crazy-quilt pattern that defied Bell's power of analysis.[31] All that he could discover was the unexceptional facts that some deaf people—he counted 607 in the United States—did indeed have deaf parents, that more than 90 percent of deaf Americans who married chose deaf partners, and that some families had a "hereditary tendency to deafness."[32] Despite Bell's failure to prove his "deaf variety" thesis, however, there continued to be pressure to force deaf people to avoid associating with, and marrying, each other.

GETTING THE DATA

The debate over deaf intermarriage in the 1880s and 1890s had one beneficial result. It led Edward Allen Fay to produce the most thorough and meticulous study of deaf marriages ever conducted. A vice president and professor of foreign languages at Gallaudet College, and for fifty years editor of the *American Annals of the Deaf*, Fay was a consummate scholar. He believed that discussions of deaf marriages and heredity needed to be supported by data. Charges by Bell and countercharges by deaf people were not clarifying anything, and they did not give deaf persons the information they needed to make wise choices in marriages. Moreover, Bell's data conflicted with information collected in other countries.[33] In 1889, Fay undertook, therefore, to record and examine the results of every marriage of deaf Americans and Canadians in the nineteenth century.

To do so, he sent out blank "marriage records" to "heads of schools for the deaf, the deaf themselves, and their relatives and friends."[34] Fay planned to use the data thus received to discover answers to four issues he believed important to help deaf people make decisions about their marriage partners: (1) Were marriages of deaf people more likely to produce deaf children than were marriages of hearing people? (2) Were marriages of two deaf people more likely to produce deaf children than were marriages of one deaf and one hearing person? (3) Were some deaf people, no matter whom they married, more likely than other people to have deaf children? (4) Were marriages of two deaf people more happy or less happy than mixed marriages of one deaf person and one hearing person?[35] An astonishingly large number of couples, 4,471, responded to Fay's questionnaires.[36]

The answers Fay received helped to quiet the panic Bell had begun. It was indeed true, Fay reported in a massive study first published in the *Annals* and then in book form by Bell's own Volta Bureau, that deaf parents were more likely than hearing parents to have deaf children. Of all marriages involving either one or two deaf partners, 9.7 percent produced deaf children, a percentage significantly above that of the general population.[37] Yet the marriages of two deaf people—the presumed cause of Bell's hypothetical "deaf variety of the human race"—were no more likely to result in deaf offspring than the marriages of one deaf person and one hearing person. Moreover, no matter whether one or two deaf people were involved in a marriage, the chances were greater than ten to one that the children would be hearing. Only 8.6 percent of the offspring of one or two deaf parents were themselves deaf.[38] Fay added one important caveat, though. His data showed that deaf persons who married relatives produced deaf children 30 percent of the time. Thus, Fay concluded, "it is exceedingly dangerous for a deaf person to marry a blood relative, no matter what the character or degree of the relationships may be, and no matter whether the relative is deaf or hearing."[39]

In light of modern knowledge of deafness and heredity, Fay's statistics are not surprising. Persons who carry a dominant gene for profound childhood deafness—a relatively rare occurrence—will, on the average, pass it to half their children no matter whom they marry.[40] Because of factors called "variable penetrance" and "expressivity," however, not all these children will actually be deaf themselves, but half will carry the gene that can cause deafness.[41] More frequently, profound childhood deafness, when related to a genetic factor, is caused by an autosomal recessive gene that affects auditory function. Because many of these exist, the chances are increased that a person who becomes deaf from this cause is the offspring of parents who are related and thus share the same recessive gene, whether or not these persons are themselves deaf.[42] Fay did not end his study with just this dry scientific information, though, for he also was interested in the happiness of deaf people.

Fay concluded that deaf adults who married other deaf people were happier, on the average, than those who married hearing persons. The rate of divorce and permanent marital separation, Fay discovered, was nearly three times greater for mixed couples than for those where both partners were deaf. Fay believed that this was due to "the strong bond of mutual fellowship growing out of their similar condition, the ease and freedom with which they communicate with each other, and the identity of their social relations and sympathies outside of the domestic circle."[43] In other words, Fay discovered what deaf Americans had come to know for themselves—that they were happiest among each other.

THE CASE OF HYPATIA BOYD REED

Innumerable examples could be given to support Fay's conclusion. A particularly telling one, however, is provided by a Wisconsin woman named Hypatia Boyd. A native of Milwaukee, Boyd lost her hearing from scarlet fever when she was six and one-half years old, after she had learned to speak and had acquired English language skills. Boyd then attended the Milwaukee Day School for the Deaf, an oral school that prohibited signing and fingerspelling. Bell and others used the Milwaukee Day School as an example of what deaf education should be. Bell had argued before the Wisconsin state legislature and elsewhere that oral day schools would lead deaf people to become integrated with the general population and to marry accordingly.[44]

Boyd seemed a perfect instance of the success of this type of education in separating deaf people from each other and preparing them for full interaction with hearing society. After graduating from the Milwaukee Day School, where she was a star pupil, she went on to attend a regular, hearing high school in Milwaukee. Relying solely on speechreading, she completed the high school course without interpreters or any other kind of special assistance. The Wisconsin Phonological Institute, a predecessor of the AAPTSD, and Bell touted Boyd's success in her Milwaukee high school as proof of what orally trained deaf people could accomplish. She did so well in the public high school that in 1895, the year of her graduation, she became the first deaf student accepted by the University of Wisconsin. Boyd attended the university for one year, again using speechreading and her own speech skills to communicate with fellow students and her instructors. Later she penned newspaper articles for Milwaukee's leading periodical, the *Milwaukee Sentinel,* and she wrote a book honoring her teacher at the Milwaukee Day School.[45] By 1900 Boyd seemed well on her way to becoming a deaf person who had prospered outside of the institutions of the deaf community and who proved the efficacy of educational methods that separated deaf people from each other.

Boyd's life took a strange turn, however. Instead of continuing her life free from the deaf community and its presumed constraints, she became a teacher at the Wisconsin School for the Deaf. In 1903 she did something even more drastic.[46] Despite her background in a day school and then in the hearing environments of a public high school and the University of Wisconsin, despite her ability to speechread easily, and despite her readily understandable voice, she married a nonspeaking, nonspeechreading, sign language–using deaf man named Reed.[47] Although Boyd's early years were presented to the public and to educators as evidence that the proper training would develop deaf individuals who were indistinguishable from the hearing population, Boyd's later experience seemed to prove otherwise. Her record typified the difficulty that hearing people would have in trying to prevent deaf people from marrying individuals with whom they shared the strongest natural bonds.

Neither the life histories of people like Boyd nor the evidence of Fay's study completely halted agitation to prevent intermarriage of deaf people. Bell continued to be concerned about this issue for the remainder of his life, and in the late twentieth century his *Memoir* with its mistaken conclusions, was reprinted and circulated by the Alexander Graham Bell Association for the Deaf without any caveats. Still, Fay's *Marriages of the Deaf* did prevent panic and quiet fears. By the early twentieth century, deaf people were able to concentrate on other matters that were becoming increasingly important to the well-being of their new community.

13

Employing the Deaf Community

During most of the nineteenth century employment had been a secondary issue for the leadership of the evolving American deaf community. Although residential schools had always offered vocational training, concerns about work did not occupy a prominent place in public debates and discussions among deaf people. One reason probably was that deaf Americans needed first to establish their educability and to throw off the yoke of paternalism that had fettered them. As long as they were fit objects for charity, jobs or careers would not be as important as they would later become. By the late nineteenth century, however, schools for deaf people had shrugged off their eleemosynary character, and deaf people had established themselves as educated and independent citizens who would be expected to support themselves, and they wanted to do so.

A second reason employment suddenly gained importance late in the nineteenth century was that economic change had revolutionized the nature of work in the United States. Farm labor and handicrafts, which had occupied most workers during the first half of the nineteenth century, required skills that could be learned without hearing. Individuals could depend on visual observation, long practice, and an intimate acquaintance with their teacher or coworkers to acquire agricultural knowledge and craftsmanship. After the Civil War, however, these kinds of occupations declined in importance to the American economy. Their place was rapidly taken by urban industrial jobs in America's new, impersonal, wage-labor factory economy.[1] Whether deaf workers could compete in the face of massive immigration and industrial policies that evaluated them as mere cogs in machines, rather than as individuals with unique skills, remained to be determined. Thus, as deaf people were defending themselves against oralists who would take away their language and forbid them from holding middle-class teaching jobs and against eugenicists who would interfere with their marriages, they realized that their economic well-being also required community attention and action.

CIVIL SERVICE STRUGGLE

The Pendleton Civil Service Act of 1883 established a new method for selecting low-level government workers. In so doing, it provided deaf people with new employment opportunities and yet increased their concern about job discrimination. Up until this time, all federal government jobs had been subject to the spoils system. Individuals received federal positions as rewards for working in support of the winning presidential candidate or party, and any person could be hired or fired at the whim of the current administration. Under the Civil Service laws, however, a three-person Civil Service Commission was given the responsibility to hire government workers on the basis of a standard civil service examination that was open to all applicants, no matter what their political party. Since deaf people usually were not politically active, except when their direct interests were involved, they had been excluded from federal jobs under the spoils system. Civil Service, therefore, seemed to provide them with an opportunity to compete for government positions.

Yet almost immediately after the Pendleton Act became law, deaf people began to worry that it discriminated against them. In 1885 the Empire State Association of Deaf-Mutes, acting on the basis of rumors (not an uncommon practice among minority groups excluded from power) appointed a committee to convince the Civil Service Commission not to prohibit deaf people from taking the examination. In response to an investigation of this issue by Edward Allen Fay, the Civil Service Commission replied that the Empire State Association did not have its facts correct. R. D. Graham, secretary of the commission, wrote that "there is no provision in the Civil Service Act or Rules which forbids the employment of deaf-mutes."[2] Indeed, this was true in practice as well as in theory, for several deaf people held Civil Service jobs during the 1880s.[3]

By the early 1890s, though, deaf people again had become concerned that the Civil Service was not allowing them to compete with hearing applicants for federal jobs. The National Association of the Deaf, meeting in Chicago in 1893, passed a resolution stating that "the rules controlling admission to the Civil Service of the Government make unfair discriminations against the deaf and deprive them of their rights as citizens." To remedy this problem, deaf people again turned to their own resources and contacted the Civil Service Commission. As earlier, they found that their information was incorrect. The Civil Service examination was open to all persons. It was true, though, that a decision of the general superintendent of the Railway Mail Service had declared, perhaps for reasons of safety, that deaf people could not be appointed to jobs in this government agency. One deaf person nevertheless advised deaf men not to seek Civil Service jobs. "Such a position," he argued, "is not the best one for an active and energetic young man."[4]

Whatever the validity of this common sentiment, deaf people were understandably alarmed when in 1906 the Civil Service adopted a regulation excluding them from federal government careers. The rule stated that persons with certain defects—such as insanity, tuberculosis, paralysis, epilepsy, blindness, and deafness—were prohibited from taking the Civil Service examination. George Veditz, Olof Hanson, and other deaf community leaders protested this discrimination in letters to the president, Theodore Roosevelt. In response, Roosevelt asked the Civil Service commissioners to explain their decision, and they responded with an odd letter on February 28, 1908.

According to the commissioners, permitting deaf people to take the examination would not be fair to them. This was true, they said, first, because few passed, and second, because only a small number of those who did pass actually received appointments to government positions, which "resulted in constant complaint from persons thus rejected, as they regarded it as a grievance that, although they had passed the test for eligibility, they were rejected after having gone to the trouble and expense of examination."[5] The confused logic of this argument, which seemed to imply that too many passed while stating that not enough passed, nevertheless swayed President Roosevelt, and he approved the commissioners' decision.[6]

Curiously, according to the Civil Service's own statistics, in 1908, 28 of the 25,000 persons employed under Civil Service classification were deaf.[7] Though this number may seem insignificant at first glance, it was not. The proportion of one deaf employee to fewer than 1,000 hearing workers was greater than the overall proportion of deaf people to hearing people in the United States, indicating that the government actually provided a disproportionately high share of jobs for deaf individuals.

Veditz, then president of the NAD, appealed the commissioners' decision, and subsequently, the commission softened its stance somewhat to allow government departments the option to permit deaf individuals to take examinations.[8] Still, this policy put an unfair burden on deaf people. They had to convince particular departments to deviate from the norm and make an exception, at their own initiative, for deaf applicants, something few departments probably were willing to do.

President William Howard Taft, who succeeded Roosevelt, took a broader view than his predecessor. In the face of pressure from Veditz, who had raised this issue with Taft while the latter was a candidate for president, and after discussions with Edward Miner Gallaudet, Taft overturned Roosevelt's decision. Taft's executive order of April 7, 1909, stated, "Deaf-mutes may be admitted to examinations for all places in the classified civil service of the United States whose duties in the opinions of the heads of the several Executive Departments they may be considered capable of performing."[9]

With this order, Taft not only reopened career opportunities for deaf people, he also acknowledged that deaf persons, as a group, should be separated from other "defectives" in the execution of some public policies. Deaf people had argued successfully that they should not be classified with people who were insane or epileptic or who suffered from contagious diseases. In this way they had asserted their uniqueness as a discrete class of Americans. Though they were different from hearing people—and they insisted on their differentness—they were not inferior or incapable of employment. In terms of career opportunities, they only wished to be treated fairly, like other American workers.

INDUSTRIAL EMPLOYMENT

The 1890 and 1900 censuses of deaf people, though not entirely accurate, indicated that the largest number of employed deaf American men were still in agricultural jobs, and most deaf women were either housewives or servants. With regard to the American deaf community, however, this data may have been somewhat misleading. The census counted all persons with a severe hearing loss as deaf, although most would not by any measure be considered members of the deaf community.[10] The incidence of deafness increases dramatically with age. Though older, deafened adults face some of the problems confronted by those who were born deaf or who lost their hearing in infancy, they do not attend deaf schools, usually do not sign, marry other deaf people, belong to deaf clubs, or in other ways identify with the deaf subculture.[11] Most of those counted in the census as deaf, therefore, probably were individuals who had spent the majority of their lives as hearing persons and then became deaf as they aged. That many of these men were involved in agriculture and many of the women were housewives, then, only indicates that the United States was still an agricultural nation in which most women did not work outside of the home, not that culturally deaf people were in 1890 and 1900 still selecting farming or being a housewife as their occupation. The employment status of persons deaf from birth or childhood, that is, members of the American deaf community, was more difficult to determine.

Beginning in 1899, however, the NAD began to study this question and others related to deaf employment in private business of all kinds. James L. Smith, president of the NAD, in December of 1899 appointed a committee of three deaf men "to collect data, etc., relating to the deaf in the industrial world." The three-member committee

Alexander L. Pach was a self-employed professional photographer in New York City. A graduate of the New York School for the Deaf, in 1899 he was appointed to an NAD committee to study deaf employment.

was composed of Warren Robinson, a teacher at the Wisconsin School for the Deaf; New York photographer Alexander Pach; and Philip Axling, a teacher at the Nebraska School for the Deaf. These three developed questionnaires and sent them to employers of deaf people, self-employed deaf businessmen, and deaf workers.[12]

The committee's findings were not dramatic. Focusing on the situation of deaf men rather than women, it discovered that most employers did not discriminate against deaf workers; that few deaf people went into business for themselves because of their inability to mingle easily with hearing people and because of deaf people's "timidity"; that deaf persons preferred working in large shops rather than small ones; that agricultural jobs were considered more attractive than factory work; and that most deaf people communicated with writing rather than with speech in their workplaces. The committee also found that deaf adults believed that schools for deaf pupils should have higher paid instructors, more modern equipment and methods, and that they needed to focus on training their students for more remunerative jobs—all recommendations with which the committee agreed.[13]

The role of residential schools in preparing deaf students for employment was a key issue, one that caused deaf persons much concern in the early twentieth century. Continuing a pattern begun in the mid-nineteenth century, the publicly supported residential institutions in the United States offered a substantial variety of vocational trades to their students. In 1907, for example, students could receive training in fifty-seven different occupations, depending upon the institutions they attended. These ranged from the very technical and equipment-intensive, such as printing, to such relatively simple and labor-intensive occupations as housework and gardening. The most common vocational skills for boys were printing, taught in forty schools, and shoemaking, taught in thirty-seven. For girls, the most frequently offered classes were dressmaking, in thirty-five institutions, and sewing, in thirty-one schools.[14] Yet despite this apparent abundance of choices, leaders had good reason for their concern about the adequacy of vocational training, as Warren Robinson shrewdly explained in 1906.

Robinson, who was then head of the NAD's Bureau of Industrial Statistics, argued that deaf people would find employment opportunities increasingly difficult in the twentieth century because of changes in the curriculum of hearing schools. Before the twentieth

In the early twentieth century, dressmaking was the most common occupation of deaf women. Here, in 1916, pupils at the Kentucky School for the Deaf learn this skill.

century, he explained, public schools for hearing students had focused almost entirely on giving their pupils academic instruction. With the influx of immigrants, the enactment of mandatory school attendance laws, the spread of so-called progressive education, and the new demands of heavy industry, however, public schools had begun to add industrial and vocational training to their course offerings. Residential school graduates previously had had an advantage over their hearing peers in career preparation, but this was no longer true. The hearing schools had caught up with the deaf schools. Thus, Robinson concluded, "the industrial question . . . is becoming more and more the question of the hour with the deaf."[15]

In addition to prodding the state residential institutions to improve their vocational education programs, deaf people took active roles in other efforts to assist themselves in finding secure employment. Articles appeared in the deaf press and in professional journals encouraging individuals to pursue particular vocations that other deaf people had found successful. Lucy Taylor of Michigan, for example, in 1909 encouraged deaf girls to learn dressmaking. A single woman

After printing, the most common industrial occupation for deaf men in 1900 was shoemaking. This is a class in shoemaking at the Maryland School for the Deaf in Frederick circa 1900.

A graduate of the Wisconsin School for the Deaf and a recipient of both Bachelor of Arts and Master of Arts degrees from Gallaudet College, Warren Robinson studied the employment status of deaf people carefully and worried that hearing children were catching up with deaf pupils in vocational training in their schools.

herself, Taylor argued that deaf females were less likely than hearing women to marry and to be able to depend on a husband to support them. They had better prepare themselves, as she had, Taylor cajoled, by mastering a trade in which hearing loss was not a disadvantage. Taylor recommended dressmaking, which allowed her independence and a comfortable income.[16] In 1908 a deaf North Carolina farmer, Robert Taylor, suggested that more deaf men should pursue farming as their career. He explained that farming was the best occupation for deaf people, not because farmers avoided social interaction in which deafness was a hindrance, but because farming was a lucrative, permanent occupation that allowed a deaf man to be free from prejudice, discrimination, or dependence.[17]

Though the Taylors provide examples of a strong self-help philosophy among deaf Americans, other deaf people tried more general means to assist their class. Deaf leaders in Minnesota were particularly active in this respect. In 1913 deaf businessman Anson Spear and others convinced the state to establish a Division of the Deaf in the Bureau of Labor and Industries.[18] Responding to pressure from his deaf constituents, Minnesota Senator Moses E. Clapp proposed as well that the federal government create a "bureau for the deaf and dumb" in the United States Department of Labor. At the suggestion of deaf Episcopal minister and school administrator James H. Cloud, the Convention of American Instructors of the Deaf in 1914 voted to recommend that Congress approve Clapp's suggestion.[19] Although this bill failed, it nevertheless demonstrated the interest and concern of the deaf community about their employment prospects as the new century began.

WAR

One of the factors that most strongly affected deaf employment in the twentieth century was war. When the United States entered World War I, the draft and increased demand for goods and services created a general shortage of American workers, and undraftable deaf men found themselves in great demand. A peculiar consequence of this was the creation of a large deaf community in Akron, Ohio.

Akron was home of the Goodyear and Firestone rubber companies, and during World War I both companies actively sought deaf factory workers to meet their demand for tire production. Firestone, pleased with its own wartime deaf workers and impressed by the experience of Goodyear with deaf laborers, in 1919 hired Ben M. Schowe, a 1918 Gallaudet College graduate, to recruit more deaf employees.[20] In the words of Gilbert Braddock, a writer for *The Silent Worker*, Firestone set out to establish "a regular colony of deaf-mutes." The company provided them with sports facilities, a dance hall, and club rooms, recognizing, as few companies or hearing individuals ever would, that deaf people were happiest when they could socialize among others who shared their language and life experiences. Braddock concluded that "this [Firestone's effort] looks good to the deaf of the whole U.S.A. . . . . It is a comfort to the able-bodied deaf man to know that he still stands a chance of getting somewhere."[21] As the twentieth century got underway, however, printing rather than making tires provided the best means of "getting somewhere."

PRINTERS:
AN INDUSTRIAL ELITE

Throughout the late nineteenth century and well into the twentieth, printing was the most important skilled occupation for deaf men. Nearly every state residential school in the United States taught printing to its male—and very occasionally its female—students.[22] Today printing may seem to be an occupation that would be reserved for

Benjamin M. Schowe, Sr., was hired by Firestone Tire and Rubber Company to recruit deaf workers after World War I.

In the early decades of the twentieth century Firestone Tire and Rubber Company of Akron, Ohio, sought deaf workers, as shown by this advertisement demonstrating the many occupations of the firm's deaf employees.

students who were not academically gifted, but that was not true for much of the history of the American deaf community. In fact, just the opposite occurred—frequently the most promising students learned printing. George Veditz and Amos Draper are two such examples. While a student at the Maryland School for the Deaf, Veditz took printing and became skilled enough to be the foreman of the institution's print shop. Yet he went on to Gallaudet College, graduated with the highest grade-point average of any student in the nineteenth century, and was accepted for graduate study at Johns Hopkins University. In 1872, Draper became a professor of Latin and mathematics at Gallaudet College, but he had studied printing while a student at the American School for the Deaf and was a professional printer in Illinois before attending college.[23]

Veditz was only one of several NAD leaders who worked as printers at some time in their careers. Fred Schreiber is probably the most noteworthy. The first executive director of the NAD, Schreiber was responsible for the evolution of that organization into a powerful national voice for deaf people. He worked for the Firestone Rubber Company in Akron as a young man, but Schreiber later turned to printing because of its greater advantages for a deaf worker.[24]

Several factors may explain the popularity of printing and its appeal to persons who were successful as students and then adults within the deaf community. One factor was the inherent power of printers in the early years of the deaf community's formation. As explained in a previous chapter, ever since the North Carolina Institution began its newspaper in 1849, school Little Papers became the primary organs through which the geographically scattered members of the deaf community kept in touch. The institution's newspaper editor thus was often an influential individual, and the editor usually was the printing instructor. Veditz, for instance, edited both the *Maryland Bulletin* and the *Colorado Index* while he taught at the Maryland and Colorado institutions.[25] The independent deaf press, too, was operated by persons who frequently combined the roles of newspaper owner, printer, and editor. Among the best known of these was Henry C. Rider, who founded the *Deaf-Mutes' Journal*, which later

Frederick C. Schreiber, one of the twentieth century's most dynamic and successful deaf leaders, was a printer for nearly twenty years.

At the outset of the twentieth century, nearly every state residential school for deaf people had a print shop similar to this one at the Maryland School for the Deaf in Frederick.

Chicagoan James E. Gallaher, editor of an excellent collective biography of nineteenth-century deaf leaders titled Representative Deaf Persons of the United States of America, *in the 1880s encouraged unusually talented deaf men to go into the printing trade because of its comparatively high wages.*

was edited by Edwin A. Hodgson, second president of the NAD, and Thomas Francis Fox, fourth president of the NAD.[26]

Another important factor was the relatively good pay that printers received. James Gallaher, who practiced the printing trade in Chicago before becoming a teacher, reported in 1880 that deaf printers could earn as much as thirty dollars a week.[27] By contrast, in 1880 American machinists and carpenters earned only about half that, and the average annual income of nonfarm workers in the United States was well below $500.[28]

The financial advantages of the printing profession continued into the twentieth century, as hearing and deaf printers were unionized, strengthening their financial position and giving them considerable job mobility. A survey of deaf printers in 1923, for instance, showed that they received an average pay of $28.50 per week, a decent wage; some linotype (a typesetting machine) operators earned up to fifty dollars per week.[29] Even in the 1930s, when the Great Depression drove down wages in nearly all industries, deaf printers reported earning as much as sixty dollars for a week's labor.

As satisfying as it may be, however, the story of deaf people's success in the printing trade is a cautionary tale as well. The nature of printing changed rapidly in the second half of the twentieth century, altering its status and reducing its importance as lucrative urban employment for deaf men. The introduction of computers and the phasing out of the old linotype machines meant that fewer workers—and workers with different skills—were needed in the printing business. Although the *Washington Post*, for example, and the Government Printing Office still employed deaf printers in the 1980s, their numbers were dwindling.

Technological change had outpaced the capacity of schools to adapt to new conditions. Furthermore, the new service-oriented economy of the United States called into question the future of deaf workers and their ability to find new employment areas in which their hearing loss would not be a competitive disadvantage. With less and less emphasis on residential schools as the primary educational institutions for deaf children, the future of the American deaf community, too, is uncertain.

14

Epilogue

The nineteenth century marked a revolution in the history of deaf people, perhaps America's most unusual minority group. Although profound questions about the methodology of deaf education remained unanswered, informed persons could no longer doubt that deaf people were educable. Deaf Americans had justified the confidence placed in them by Laurent Clerc, Thomas Hopkins Gallaudet, and Mason Fitch Cogswell. Most who had entered schools had succeeded in acquiring elementary and secondary educations. Some had graduated from college, and a few had achieved graduate and professional degrees. During the nineteenth century, however, this oppressed group of individuals had accomplished something else as well, something revolutionary, and something unforeseen by Gallaudet, Cogswell, and other hearing persons.

Beginning the century as isolated individuals, coming from diverse ethnic and regional backgrounds, and usually raised by parents whose culture they would never share completely, deaf people had fashioned a subculture and a community that paralleled those of immigrant groups and that satisfied the particular needs of persons who were deaf. Deaf Americans welcomed the twentieth century with their own visual language, their own churches and ministers, their own clubs and associations, and their own newspapers. Like members of the most closely knit ethnic groups, they married each other almost exclusively. They had withstood challenges to the legitimacy of their culture and to their right to form a group within yet apart from hearing society.

They had not done so alone. Sympathetic and astute hearing persons had opened doors, raised money for educational efforts, and helped provide a link between the deaf world and a hearing society whose members could not comprehend the significance of deafness or realize the potential of deaf people to function without the normal channels of human communication. Often these hearing people were motivated by religious calling, as were Thomas Hopkins Gallaudet and many of the first teachers and administrators in residential schools. Others, like Mason Fitch Cogswell, Edward Miner Gallaudet, E. S. Tillinghast, and even Alexander Graham Bell, had deaf individuals in their families and thus knew them intimately. By the end of the nineteenth century, though, the hearing people involved with deafness on a daily basis were most often professionals, teachers or administrators, who had chosen to develop careers based on expertise in the area of deafness. Fortunately for deaf people, individuals from their own ranks rose to the leadership of their new community as "helping the deaf" became a profession rather than a calling.

The earliest deaf leaders were all adventitiously deaf. Olof Hanson, Edmund Booth, Edwin Hodgson, George Veditz, J. Schuyler Long, and Robert McGregor, to name a few, all became deaf long after they had learned to read, write, and speak English. They were relatively comfortable in either the deaf or the hearing community, and thus, like leaders of all minority groups in American history, they were able to form a bridge from the dominant majority to the oppressed minority that they represented.[1] As the nineteenth century ended, these individuals and dozens like them helped create the institutions, the communications networks, and the community infrastructure that helped prepare other deaf people for the years that lay ahead. And innumerable challenges still confronted deaf Americans. In the twentieth century they would continue the fight to gain self-determination over important aspects of their lives. Proving the value of sign language, especially in educational settings, would be a seemingly endless struggle. Deaf people would fend off attempts to deny them the right to drive automobiles.[2] They would work to gain civil rights, such as the right to serve on juries, to be adequately represented in courts, to have access to television and to higher education, and to be heard in debates over public policies that might affect them.[3] By the late 1980s these problems still were not resolved to the total satisfaction of many within the deaf community, and new threats loomed.

Perhaps the most serious of these was the Education for All Handicapped Children Act of 1975. This seemingly benign amendment to an earlier law authorizing federal support for programs to benefit handicapped children, required that handicapped children be educated in the "least restrictive environment."[4] This could be interpreted to mean that deaf children should not be placed in residential schools with other deaf students. Whatever the educational value of such an effort, it struck at the heart of the institution most responsible for socializing deaf children into the adult deaf community. It was in the residential schools that deaf Americans first met each other, developed a standard visual language, and discovered the common interests that presaged the formation of their community.

Still, the future of the deaf community is not bleak. Its history has shown that deaf people realize that in community they have strength. If they understand that history and heed its lessons, they will be able to unite to define their interests again and to preserve their victories, refashioning their objectives and their methods to meet the new conditions of the twentieth and twenty-first centuries. One indication that they will do so was the Deaf President Now strike that paralyzed Gallaudet University in the spring of 1988 and brought about a revolution in that venerable institution's leadership.

DEAF PRESIDENT NOW

On Monday, March 7, 1988, Gallaudet University students seized control of the campus, barricading its side entrances with their parked cars and the main entrance with their bodies. All campus activities halted. Classes were not held; most faculty, staff, and administrators stayed away; and a festival atmosphere took over. For the remainder of the week the campus remained under control of the strikers. The main administration building, named for the university's first president, Edward Miner Gallaudet, was sealed shut with students' hardened-steel bicycle locks. Students and their supporters among the faculty, staff, and the wider deaf community demonstrated, raised some $25,000 to support the costs of the strike, marched to the Capitol, and drew the attention of America's national media to the besieged—yet calm—campus.[5]

DPN, as the Deaf President Now strike or movement was commonly called, had four overt objectives. First, it sought to overturn a

March 6 decision of the university's Board of Trustees to name Elisabeth Ann Zinser, a hearing woman with no previous knowledge of
the deaf community, the university's seventh president. Students demanded that one of the two deaf finalists, Harvey Corson, superintendent of the Louisiana School for the Deaf, or Irving King Jordan,
Jr., dean of Gallaudet University's College of Arts and Sciences, be
selected in place of Zinser. Second, DPN leaders insisted that Jane
Bassett Spilman, the chairman of the Board of Trustees, resign from
the board. The third demand was that 51 percent of the members of
the Board of Trustees be deaf themselves. Fourth, and finally, students insisted that they would close the campus until the administration promised that there would be no reprisals against the students,
faculty, administrators, or staff who had taken part in the strike.[6]
Remarkably, considering the limited success of student protest movements of the 1960s, all these demands (except immediate implementa-
tion of the demand for a 51 percent deaf Board of Trustees) were met.

On March 10 Zinser resigned from her three-day-old presidency
of Gallaudet, stating that DPN represented "an extraordinary social
movement of deaf people" and "a civil rights movement in history for
deaf people."[7] On Sunday, March 13, one week after the board's initial decision that sparked the DPN strike, the Board of Trustees met
again. In a day-long session board chairman Spilman resigned; Philip
Bravin, one of the four deaf members of the board, was named the
new chairman; and Irving King Jordan, Jr., was selected as the first
deaf president in Gallaudet University's history.[8]

A full account of DPN is beyond the scope of this work, but
even a brief analysis indicates that the strike and its outcome have
meaning for the deaf community on several levels. The activities of
the students and their supporters showed dramatically that in the
1980s deaf people could be galvanized to unite around a common
issue, particularly one with great symbolic meaning, such as the Gallaudet presidency. Gallaudet University represents the pinnacle of education for deaf people, not only in the United States but throughout
the world. The assumption of its presidency by a person himself deaf
announced to the world that deaf Americans were now a mature minority. Like black people or women, deaf people now have their most
important and most visible educational institution headed by one of
them. Although issues of communication and assimilation may divide
deaf people, they coalesced in their belief that a deaf person could
and should be Gallaudet University's president.

The strike also proved that by the late 1980s deaf Americans had learned how to manipulate the mass media to their advantage. DPN activists prepared press kits for television and newspaper reporters. They established a media center at the main campus entrance to distribute information and propaganda and to arrange interviews, while hearing volunteers staffed a telephone bank in the alumni house to handle phone requests for news. The student leaders, who appeared endlessly on local and national television, disdained oral speech—though some have readily understandable voices—and used signs. Though this could have presented severe problems, for few viewers understand American Sign Language, the strike leaders turned their language to their own advantage. Highly skilled interpreters were recruited to translate simultaneously the students' signs into spoken language for hearing television viewers. Thus the students could speak in a language in which they were articulate, comfortable, and relaxed, yet hearing people also could understand them and appreciate the power and intelligence behind the signs. One profound effect of this was to demonstrate, before a huge audience, just how inappropriate it was for a nonsigning, hearing president to try to govern the university. The clear message was twofold: first, that the dominant language on the campus, and among the American deaf community, was signs; and, second, that most deaf people do not lack language skills; many just lack the ability to articulate English clearly.

The ultimate choice of Irving King Jordan, Jr., as president again revealed how much deaf Americans have in common with other minorities. In keeping with the tradition of minority leadership, Jordan is thoroughly bicultural. He possessed normal hearing until he was twenty-one years old, when a motorcycle accident left him deaf. Unlike most students and adults in the deaf community, Jordan has a hearing spouse and speaks clear, appropriately modulated and inflected English. A Gallaudet graduate, he signs fluently and is a nationally recognized scholar in the field of the psycholinguistics of sign language, which he studied while earning graduate degrees in psychology at the University of Tennessee. Jordan, therefore, moves easily and confidently in either the culture of hearing Americans or in the culture of those who do not hear. Yet he is deaf, and that fact is of overwhelming importance to the deaf community.

DPN, then, was clearly in the mainstream of the history of American deaf activism. It demonstrated that the principles of deaf self-determination that played such an important role after the first two decades of the nineteenth century were still important in the late twentieth century. The impetus for reform and change came from deaf people themselves. They began, led, and brought the strike to a successful conclusion. With similar unity in the future, they may move into a position of full equality with their hearing compatriots.

Notes

ABBREVIATIONS USED FREQUENTLY IN THE ENDNOTES

AGB Alexander Graham Bell

Annals *American Annals of the Deaf*

FP Alexander Graham Bell Family Papers, Manuscript Division, Library of Congress, Washington, D.C.

GEDPD John V. Van Cleve, ed., *Gallaudet Encyclopedia of Deaf People and Deafness*, 3 vols. (New York: McGraw-Hill, 1987)

GUA Gallaudet University Archives, Gallaudet University, Washington, D.C.

MFC Mason Fitch Cogswell Collection, Beineke Memorial Library, Yale University, New Haven, Connecticut

THG Thomas Hopkins Gallaudet Collection, Library of Congress, Manuscript Division, Washington, D.C.

TFP Tillinghast Family Papers, William R. Perkins Library, Duke University, Durham, North Carolina

CHAPTER 1

1. Pierre Desloges' book, *Observations d'un sourd et muet sur 'Un Cours élémentaire d'éducation des sourds et muets,' publie en 1779 par M. L'abbé Deschamps*, is translated in Harlan Lane, ed., *The Deaf Experience: Classics in Language and Education*, trans. Franklin Philip (Cambridge: Harvard University Press, 1984), 28–48.

2. Nora Groce, *Everyone Here Spoke Sign Language: Hereditary Deafness on Martha's Vineyard* (Cambridge: Harvard University Press, 1985), 4, 79.

3. All quotations are from the King James Version of the Bible.

4. Harvey P. Peet, "Memoir on the Origin and Early History of the Art of Instructing the Deaf and Dumb," *Annals* 3 (April 1851): 135; Stephen Klopfer, *St. Augustine and the Deaf* (Columbus, Ohio: Catholic Educational Association, n.d.), 5; Felix Zillmann, *Saint Augustine and the Education of the Deaf*, trans. S. Klopfer, reprint from *Our Young People—The Deaf-Mutes' Friend* 41, nos. 11 and 12; 42, nos. 1 and 2; 1–3.

5. Klopfer, *Augustine*, 6–7.

6. Quoted in Edward Allen Fay, "What Did St. Augustine Say?" *Annals* 57 (January 1912): 119.

7. Quoted in Hans Werner, *History of the Problem of Deaf-Mutism Until the Seventeenth Century*, trans. C. K. Bonning (Jena: n.p., 1932), 39.

8. Ibid., 47–48.

9. Quoted in ibid., 74–75.

10. Ynez Viole O'Neill, *Speech and Speech Disorders in Western Thought Before 1600* (Westport, Conn.: Greenwood Press, 1980), 198–201.

11. Quoted in Werner, *Deaf-Mutism*, 183–184.

CHAPTER 2

1. Hans Werner, *History of the Problem of Deaf-Mutism until the Seventeenth Century*, trans. C. K. Bonning (Jena: n.p., 1932), 364, 375–378, 382.

2. Juan Pablo Bonet, *Simplification of the Letters of the Alphabet and Method of Teaching Deaf-Mutes to Speak*, trans. H. N. Dixon (London: Hazell, Watson, and Viney, 1890).

3. Ibid., 154.

4. Ibid., 197–198.

5. Ibid., 199.

6. Ibid., 200.

7. Ibid., 200–201.

8. Ibid., 202–203.

9. Ibid., 203.

10. Kenelm Digby, *Of Bodies, and of Man's Soul* (London: John Williams, 1669), 319–320.

11. Ibid., 321. Digby's account appeared earlier in John Bulwer, *Philocophus, or, the deaf and dumbe man's friend* . . . (London: H. Moseley, 1648), 56–61.

12. George Sibscota, trans., *The Deaf and Dumb Man's Discourse* by Anthony Deusing (London: William Crook, 1670), 41.

13. Ibid., 41.

14. Charlotte Baker-Shenk, "Sign Languages: Facial Expressions," *GEDPD*, 3: 37–42.

15. Sibscota, *Deaf and Dumb*, 41.

16. Ibid., 43.

17. Ibid., 43–45.

18. AGB, "Historical Notes Concerning the Teaching of Speech to the Deaf," *Association Review* 2 (February 1900): 36.

19. Samuel A. Green, "The Earliest Advocate of the Education of Deaf-Mutes in America," *Annals* 13 (March 1861): 3.

20. John Harrower, "Documents: Diary of John Harrower, 1773–1776," *American Historical Review* 6 (October 1900): 65–71.

21. Ibid., 72.

22. Ibid., 78.

23. Ibid., 81–82.

24. Ibid., 88.

25. Ibid., 93, 95.

CHAPTER 3

1. Wyndham Robertson and R. A. Brook, *Pocahontas, Alias Matoaka, and Her Descendants . . .* (Baltimore, Md.: Genealogical Publishing Company, 1982), 31.

2. Ibid., 60.

3. Both letters were reprinted in the *National Deaf-Mute Gazette* 1 (November 1867): 14.

4. Thomas Braidwood *v.* Thomas Bolling, Federal Circuit Court, Ended Cases (unrestored), B–C, Box 39, 1797, Virginia State Library, Richmond, Va.

5. Ibid.

6. William Bolling to John Braidwood, March 17, 1812, William Bolling Letterbook, Valentine Museum, Richmond, Va.

7. Job Williams, "A Brief History of the American Asylum at Hartford for the Education and Instruction of the Deaf and Dumb," p. 10, in Edward Allen Fay, ed., *Histories of American Schools for the Deaf, 1817–1893* (Washington, D.C.: Volta Bureau, 1893), vol. 1: Sylvester Gilbert to Mason Fitch Cogswell, March 1812, MFC.

8. Mason F. Cogswell to John Braidwood, April 20, 1812, in Grace Cogswell Root, ed., *Father and Daughter: A Collection of Cogswell Family Letters and Diaries* (West Hartford, Conn.: American School for the Deaf, 1924), 66–67.

9. Bolling to Braidwood, March 17, 1812, Bolling Letterbook, Valentine Museum.

10. John Braidwood to William Bolling, April 1, 1812, Bolling Family Papers, William R. Perkins Library, Duke University, Durham, N.C.

11. *Richmond Enquirer*, June 2, 1812, p. 1.

12. *Richmond Enquirer*, February 15, 1815, p. 1.

13. "William Albert Bolling Manuscript School Book," Volta Bureau, Washington, D.C. Marcus Flournoy was the brother of John Jacobus Flournoy, who figured prominently in one of the deaf community's greatest controversies. See chapter 6.

14. Robertson and Brook, *Pocahontas*, 32.

15. Thomas Jefferson to Joseph C. Cabbell, January 24, 1816, in *Early History of the University of Virginia, as Contained in the Letters of Thomas Jefferson and Joseph C. Cabell* (Richmond, Va.: J. W. Randolph, 1856), 49.

16. *Richmond Enquirer*, June 27, 1817, p. 4.

CHAPTER 4

1. Job Williams, "A Brief History of the American Asylum at Hartford for the Education and Instruction of the Deaf and Dumb," p. 12, in Edward Allen Fay, ed., *Histories of American Schools for the Deaf, 1817–1893* (Washington, D.C.: Volta Bureau, 1893), vol. 1.

2. Paul Mattingly, "History: Deafness and Reform," *GEDPD*, 2: 46.

3. Williams, "American Asylum," 12–13.

4. Ibid., 22.

5. Melanie Yeager Williams, "Alice Cogswell," *GEDPD*, 1: 196.

6. Williams "American Asylum," 9.

7. Sylvester Gilbert to Mason Fitch Cogswell, March 1812, MFC.

8. Daniel Wadsworth, William Ely, and Henry Hudson, *First Report of the Connecticut Asylum for the Education and Instruction of Deaf and Dumb Persons* (Hartford, Conn.: n.p., 1817), 7.

9. Eliphalet Kimball to Mason Fitch Cogswell, January 4, 1814, MFC.

10. James J. Fernandes, "Thomas Hopkins Gallaudet," *GEDPD*, 1: 445.

11. Ibid., 445.

12. Donald F. Moores, *Educating the Deaf: Psychology, Principles, and Practices* (Boston: Houghton Mifflin, 1982), 56.

13. Harlan Lane, *When the Mind Hears: A History of the Deaf* (New York: Random House, 1984), 158.

14. Henry Barnard, "Thomas Hopkins Gallaudet: Eulogy," *Annals* 4 (January 1852): 89.

15. Thomas Hopkins Gallaudet to Mason Fitch Cogswell, July 11, 1815, THG.

16. Thomas Hopkins Gallaudet to Alice Cogswell, March 24, 1816, THG.

17. Thomas Hopkins Gallaudet to Abbé Sicard, May 21, 1816, THG.

18. William W. Turner, "Laurent Clerc," *Annals* 15 (January 1870): 15.

19. Gallaudet to Sicard, May 21, 1816, THG.

20. Abbé Sicard said that Clerc was "slightly acquainted with the English language." L'abbé Sicard to John Cheverus, June 16, 1816, Laurent Clerc Collection, Sterling Memorial Library, Yale University, New Haven, Conn.

21. Lane, *Mind*, 16.

22. Thomas Hopkins Gallaudet and Laurent Clerc, "Contract Between Gallaudet and Clerc, 1816," *Annals* 24 (April 1879): 115.

23. Ibid., 116–117.

24. Ibid., 115–116.

25. Ibid., 116.

26. Ibid., 117.

27. Ibid.

28. Thomas Hopkins Gallaudet to Mason Fitch Cogswell, June 17, 1816, reprinted in Grace Cogswell Root, ed., *Father and Daughter: A Collection of Cogswell Family Letters and Diaries* (West Hartford, Conn.: American School for the Deaf, 1924), 69.

29. Thomas Hopkins Gallaudet to Mason Fitch Cogswell, August 10, 1816, MFC.

30. Clerc's letter was contained in Gallaudet to Cogswell, August 10, 1816, THG.

31. Alice Cogswell to Thomas Hopkins Gallaudet, December 27, 1816, THG.

32. Williams, "American Asylum," 11; Gallaudet's use of religious arguments to develop financial support for deaf education can be seen in one of his most frequently used speeches: *Sermon on the Duty and Advantages of Affording Instruction to the Deaf and Dumb* (Concord, Mass.: Isaac Hill, 1824).

33. E. H. Currier and Thomas F. Fox, "New York Institution for the Instruction of the Deaf and Dumb," p. 11, in Fay, ed., *Histories*, vol. 1.

34. Laurent Clerc to Mason Fitch Cogswell, January, 1817, MFC.

35. Currier and Fox, "New York Institution," 12.

36. Williams, "American Asylum," 13.

37. Nina Fletcher Little, "John Brewster, Jr.," *GEDPD*, 1: 156–157.

38. Wadsworth et al., *Report*, 7.

39. For the origins of American Sign Language, see Harlan Lane, "Sign Languages: American, History," *GEDPD*, 3: 53–56.

40. Seth Terry, *Third Report of the Directors of the Connecticut Asylum for the Education and Instruction of Deaf and Dumb Persons* (Hartford, Conn.: Hudson and Company, 1819), 6.

41. Ibid., 7.

42. Ibid., 8.

43. Wadsworth et al., *Report*, 5.

CHAPTER 5

1. Edward Allen Fay, ed., *Histories of American Schools for the Deaf, 1817–1893* (Washington, D.C.: Volta Bureau, 1893), vol. 1.

2. Eustachian tube dysfunction related to hearing loss and modern surgical procedures are discussed in Werner D. Chasin, "The Clinical Management of Otologic Disorders," in Larry J. Bradford and William G. Hardy, eds., *Hearing and Hearing Impairment* (New York: Grune and Stratton, 1979), 97–98.

3. J. H. Norwood to Samuel W. Tillinghast, August 9, 1836, TFP.

4. E. H. Currier and Thomas Fox, "New York Institution for the Instruction of the Deaf and Dumb," pp. 16–18, 28, in Fay, ed., *Histories*, vol. 1.

5. Norwood to Tillinghast, August 9, 1836, TFP.

6. Jn. I. Pasteur to Samuel W. Tillinghast, December 30, 1841, TFP.

7. In 1984 Alabama, Arizona, Colorado, Florida, Hawaii, Montana, South Carolina, Utah, Virginia, and West Virginia had combined residential schools for deaf students and blind students. "Schools and Class for the Deaf in the United States," *Annals* 130 (April 1985): 81–129.

8. Thomas S. Doyle, "The Virginia Institution for the Education of the Deaf and Dumb (and of the Blind)," p. 7, in Fay, ed., *Histories*, vol. 1.

9. Edmund Booth, "Rev. Joseph Dennis Tyler," *American Era* 31 (January 1945): 37–39.

10. Doyle, "The Virginia Institution," 7–8.

11. Margaret Eckridge to Robina Norwood, May 26, 1842, TFP.

12. Joseph D. Tyler to Samuel W. Tillinghast, November 1, 1842, TFP.

13. Thomas H. Tillinghast to Jane Tillinghast, April 9, 1846, TFP.

14. Tyler to Tillinghast, November 1, 1842.

15. Ibid.

16. Ibid.

17. Thomas H. Tillinghast to Samuel and Jane Tillinghast, November 2, 1842, TFP.

18. Joseph D. Tyler to Samuel W. Tillinghast, March 6, 1843, TFP.

19. Thomas H. Tillinghast to Jane Tillinghast, October 11, 1844, TFP.

20. Joseph D. Tyler to Samuel W. Tillinghast, October 11, 1844, TFP.

21. Samuel W. Tillinghast to Thomas H. Tillinghast, October 16, 1845, TFP.

22. D. McK. Goodwin, "The North Carolina Institution for the Deaf and Dumb and Blind," p. 7, in Fay, ed., *Histories*, vol. 1.

23. "David Ray Tillinghast," in James E. Gallaher, ed., *Representative Deaf Persons of the United States of America* (Chicago: James E. Gallaher, 1898), 180–181.

CHAPTER 6

1. Newell G. Bringhurst, *Brigham Young and the Expanding American Frontier* (Boston: Little Brown, 1986), 73–75.

2. Perry Miller, *Errand into the Wilderness* (New York: Harper and Row, 1956), 4–5.

3. See Edwin S. Redkey, *Black Exodus: Black Nationalist and Back-to-Africa Movements, 1890–1910* (New Haven, Conn.: Yale University Press, 1969).

4. Douglas Bullard, *Islay* (Silver Spring, Md.: T. J. Publishers, 1986).

5. Barry A. Crouch, "Alienation and the Mid-Nineteenth Century American Deaf Community: A Response," *Annals* 131 (December 1986): 322–323.

6. William W. Turner to J. J. Flournoy, December 6, 1855, published in "Scheme for a Commonwealth," *Annals* 8 (January 1856): 118.

7. Ibid.

8. Ibid., 119–120.

9. J. J. Flournoy to William W. Turner, December 21, 1855, in "Scheme," 121.

10. Ibid., 123–125.

11. John V. Van Cleve, "Edmund Booth," GEDPD, 1: 143–144.

12. Booth's encounters with deaf people on his sojourn to California are discussed in his Edmund Booth, Forty-Niner (Stockton, Calif.: San Joaquin Pioneer and Historical Society, 1953).

13. Edmund Booth to John J. Flournoy, September 6, 1857, published in "Mr. Flournoy's Plan for a Deaf-Mute Commonwealth," Annals 10 (January 1858): 40–42.

14. William Chamberlain, "Mr. Chamberlain and others on Mr. Flournoy's Project," Annals 10 (April 1858): 88–89.

15. Francis C. Higgins, "John Carlin," GEDPD, 1: 178.

16. Edward Miner Gallaudet, History of the College for the Deaf, 1857–1907, ed. Lance J. Fischer and David de Lorenzo (Washington, D.C.: Gallaudet College Press, 1983), 48.

17. P. H. Confer to Samuel Porter Chamberlain, "Mr. Chamberlain and others," Annals 10 (April 1858): 87–88.

18. William Chamberlain, "Proceedings of the Third Convention of the New England Gallaudet Association of Deaf-Mutes," Annals 10 (October 1858): 212–213, 215.

19. Ibid., 214–215.

20. For an alternative interpretation of the meaning of the deaf commonwealth debate, see Margaret Winzer, "Deaf-Mutia: Responses to Alienation by the Deaf in Mid-Nineteenth Century America," Annals 131 (March 1986): 29–32.

21. T. R. Armitage to AGB, May 19, 1883, FP.

22. Quoted in A Future for the Deaf and Dumb in the Canadian North-West (London: Potter Brothers, 1884), 9–12.

23. Canadian Department of Agriculture to AGB, July 16, 1885, FP. See also "Notices of Publications," Annals 31 (January 1886): 63–64, and "The Manitoba Colonists," Annals 31 (July 1886): 228.

CHAPTER 7

1. Edward Allen Fay, ed., Histories of American Schools for the Deaf, 1817–1893 (Washington, D.C.: Volta Bureau, 1893), vols. 1, 2.

2. See chapter 13 for a more complete discussion of technical training in schools for deaf pupils.

3. For example, Milwaukee, Wis., a good-sized city, opened its first public high school in 1868. Robert C. Nesbit, Wisconsin: A History (Madison: University of Wisconsin Press, 1973), 345.

4. Edward C. Merrill, Jr., "Gallaudet College," GEDPD, 1: 448.

5. Nineteen of the first twenty-three presidents of the National Association

of the Deaf attended Gallaudet College; two attended other colleges; and two did not attend any postsecondary programs. Jack Gannon, *Deaf Heritage: A Narrative History of Deaf America* (Silver Spring, Md.: National Association of the Deaf, 1981), 422–423.

6. Edward Miner Gallaudet, *History of the College for the Deaf, 1857–1907*, ed. Lance J. Fischer and David de Lorenzo (Washington, D.C.: Gallaudet College Press, 1983), 64.

7. John V. Van Cleve, "Edward Allen Fay," *GEDPD*, 1: 427.

8. John B. Hotchkiss, who began teaching in 1869, and Amos Draper, who started in 1872, were the first deaf faculty. Edward Miner Gallaudet, "The Columbia Institution for the Instruction of the Deaf and Dumb," in Fay, *Histories*, vol. 2.

9. Jacob Van Nostrand, "Necessity of a Higher Standard of Education for the Deaf and Dumb," *Annals* 3 (July 1851): 196–197.

10. Ibid., 197–198.

11. Ibid., 197.

12. Ibid., 198.

13. John Carlin, "Advantages and Disadvantages of the Use of Signs," *Annals* 4 (October 1851): 49.

14. Ibid., 50.

15. John Carlin, "The National College for Mutes," *Annals* 6 (April 1854): 178.

16. Ibid., 176–177.

17. Ibid., 177–178.

18. For biographical information see Francis C. Higgins, "John Kitto," *GEDPD*, 2: 129–131; William Moody, "Jean-Ferdinand Berthier," *GEDPD*, 1: 141–143; and Taras B. Denis, "James Nack," *GEDPD*, 2: 119–120.

19. Carlin, "National College," 179–180.

20. David de Lorenzo, "Edward Miner Gallaudet," *GEDPD*, 1: 439.

21. Gallaudet, *History*, 5.

22. de Lorenzo, "Gallaudet," 440.

23. Robert V. Remini, *Andrew Jackson and the Course of American Freedom, 1822–1832* (New York: Harper and Row, 1981), 127–128, 327.

24. Samuel Eliot Morison, *The Oxford History of the American People* (New York: Oxford University Press, 1965), 454.

25. de Lorenzo, "Gallaudet," 440.

26. Amos Kendall to Edward M. Gallaudet, May 14, 1857, published in Gallaudet, *History*, 6–7.

27. Ibid.

28. Ibid., 7.

29. Edward M. Gallaudet to Amos Kendall, May 18, 1857, published in ibid., 7–9.

30. Ibid., 11.

31. Ibid., 19–24, 28–31.

32. For a detailed discussion of organizational changes in the school's early years, see Gallaudet, "The Columbia Institution," pp. 3–7, in Fay, ed., *Histories*, vol. 2.

33. Ibid., 14.

34. Ibid., 8–9.

35. John Carlin, "Oration: A College for the Deaf and Dumb," June 28, 1864, published in *Seventh Annual Report of the Columbia Institution for the Deaf and Dumb and the Blind* (Washington, D.C.: n.p., 1864), 28–33.

36. Edward Miner Gallaudet, *Eighth Annual Report of the Columbia Institution for the Deaf and Dumb* (Washington, D.C.: n.p., 1865), 5–6.

37. Ibid., 6.

38. Ibid., 8.

39. Ibid., 7.

40. Gallaudet, *History*, 166–167.

CHAPTER 8

1. See Paul C. Higgins, *Outsiders in a Hearing World: A Sociology of Deafness* (Beverly Hills, Calif.: Sage Publications, 1980).

2. Frank B. Sullivan, "National Fraternal Society of the Deaf," *GEDPD*, 2: 224–227.

3. Jerome Schein, "National Association of the Deaf," *GEDPD*, 2: 220–221.

4. William M. Chamberlain, "Proceedings of the Convention of the New England Gallaudet Association of Deaf-Mutes," *Annals* 9 (April 1857): 78–79.

5. "Constitution of the New England Gallaudet Association of Deaf Mutes," published in ibid., 78–82.

6. Ibid., 67.

7. William M. Chamberlain, "Proceedings of the Board of Managers of the 'New England Gallaudet Association of Deaf-Mutes,'" *Annals* 11 (October 1859): 211.

8. Jack Gannon, *Deaf Heritage: A Narrative History of Deaf America* (Silver Spring, Md.: National Association of the Deaf, 1981), 238–239.

9. Chamberlain, "Proceedings of the Convention," 82–87.

10. Quoted in H. C. Rider, "Elmira Convention of Deaf Mutes," *Annals* 22 (October 1877): 251.

11. See chapter 10.

12. Schein, "National Association," 220.

13. Gannon, *Deaf Heritage*, 62.

14. Angelina Fuller Fischer, "Edmund Booth," in J. E. Gallaher, ed., *Representative Deaf Persons of the United States of America* (Chicago: James E. Gallaher, 1898), 11.

15. Theodore A. Froehlich, "Importance of Association Among Mutes for

Mutual Improvement," *Proceedings of the First National Convention of Deaf-Mutes* (New York: New York Institution for the Deaf and Dumb, 1880), 39.

16. Ibid., 40.

17. David Greene, "The Institution for the Improved Instruction of Deaf-Mutes," p. 3, in Edward Allen Fay, ed., *Histories of American Schools for the Deaf, 1817–1893* (Washington, D.C.: Volta Bureau, 1893), vol. 2.

18. Pamphlet by Samuel Frankenheim, published as "History of the Deaf-Mutes' Union League," *Deaf-Mutes' Journal* 35 (January 11, 1906): 1.

19. Gannon, *Deaf Heritage*, 67.

20. Frankenheim, "Union League," 1.

CHAPTER 9

1. Jack Gannon, *Deaf Heritage: A Narrative History of Deaf America* (Silver Spring, Md.: National Association of the Deaf, 1981), 247.

2. Edward Allen Fay, ed., *Histories of American Schools for the Deaf, 1817–1893* (Washington, D.C.: Volta Bureau, 1893), 3: appendix.

3. John V. Van Cleve, "Little Paper Family," *GEDPD*, 2: 193.

4. Arkansas *Optic*, October 17, 1891, GUA.

5. "Beer and Tobacco," *The Silent Worker* 2 (December 20, 1888): 1.

6. Van Cleve, "Little Paper Family," 194.

7. *The Silent Worker*, 5 (May 26, 1892).

8. John V. Van Cleve, "Nebraska's Oral Law of 1911 and the Deaf Community," *Nebraska History* 65 (Summer 1984): 205–206.

9. Ibid., 208.

10. "Dr. Gillett to Mr. Bell," *The Silent Worker* 4 (November 27, 1890): 1,4.

11. "Intermarriage Again," *The Silent Worker* 4 (December 25, 1890): 1.

CHAPTER 10

1. "Tabular Statement of American Schools for the Deaf, October 20, 1920," *Annals* 66 (January 1921): 36–37.

2. AGB, "Fallacies Concerning the Deaf," *Annals* 29 (January 1884): 32–60; AGB, *Memoir upon the Formation of a Deaf Variety of the Human Race* (Washington, D.C.: Government Printing Office, 1884).

3. Robert Harmon, "Samuel Heinicke," *GEDPD*, 2: 35–38.

4. Robert C. Spencer, "The Wisconsin System of Public Day Schools," p. 4, in Edward Allen Fay, ed., *Histories of American Schools for the Deaf, 1817–1893* (Washington, D.C.: Volta Bureau, 1893), vol. 3.

5. Rene Bernard, "Abbé Charles Michel de l'Épée," *GEDPD*, 1: 416–417.

6. C. W. Saegert, "Education of the Deaf and Dumb in Prussia," trans. Benjamin Talbot, *Annals* 9 (October 1857): 218–219.

7. Harlan Lane, *When the Mind Hears: A History of the Deaf* (New York: Random House, 1984), 377–380; "How to Teach Deaf Mutes," *Philadelphia Sun,* June 29, 1896.

8. John V. Van Cleve, "History: Congress of Milan," *GEDPD,* 2: 63–64.

9. Ibid., 65.

10. Edward Miner Gallaudet, "The Milan Convention," *Annals* 26 (January 1881): 4.

11. Quoted in ibid., 5–6.

12. Quoted in ibid., 2.

13. Quoted in ibid., 4.

14. Van Cleve, "Milan," 67.

15. See, for example, Lewis Weld, "The American Asylum," *Annals* 1 (January 1848): 107–108.

16. For a more detailed history, see F. B. Sanborn, "The Clarke Institution for Deaf Mutes," pp. 6–13, in Fay, ed., *Histories,* vol. 2.

17. Edward Miner Gallaudet, "The American System of Deaf-Mute Instruction—Its Incidental Defects and Their Remedies," *Annals* 13 (September 1868): 168.

18. John V. Van Cleve, "George William Veditz," *GEDPD,* 3: 334.

19. Robert V. Bruce, *Bell: Alexander Graham Bell and the Conquest of Solitude* (Boston: Little, Brown, 1973), 20–22.

20. AGB to Alexander Melville Bell, May 1871, FP.

21. AGB to his parents, December 1, 1871, FP.

22. James E. Gallaher, ed., *Representative Deaf Persons of the United States of America* (Chicago: James E. Gallaher, 1898), 100.

23. AGB to parents, December 1, 1871, FP.

24. AGB to Alexander Melville Bell, May 1871, FP.

25. Alexander Graham Bell's Lesson Book for September 1871, FP.

26. AGB to parents, December 1, 1871, FP.

27. Ibid.

28. AGB to parents, April 17, 1872, FP.

29. AGB to parents, January 1, 1872, FP.

30. Robert C. Spencer to AGB, April 18, 1884, FP.

31. A. J. Winnie, comp., *History and Handbook of Day Schools for the Deaf and Blind* (Madison, Wis.: Democrat Printing Company, 1912), 11.

32. AGB to Mabel Gardiner Bell, February 16, 1885, FP.

33. Edward Allen Fay, "Day-Schools in Wisconsin," *Annals* 30 (October 1885): 302.

34. "Individual Histories of Day Schools for the Deaf," in Winnie, comp., *History and Handbook,* 32–73.

35. Robert C. Spencer to AGB, April 28, 1900, reprinted in *Association Review* 2 (June 1900): 255.

36. Edward Allen Fay, "Day Schools," *Annals 44* (September 1899): 395–396; Edward Allen Fay, "Day Schools in California," *Annals* 48 (May 1903): 304.

37. Robert C. Spencer to AGB, December 29, 1883, FP.

38. AGB to Mabel Gardiner Bell, July 11, 1897, FP.

39. Edgar B. Wesley, *NEA: The First Hundred Years* (New York: Harper and Brothers, 1957), 186–187.

40. Quoted in John V. Van Cleve, "Nebraska's Oral Law of 1911 and the Deaf Community," *Nebraska History* 65 (Summer 1984): 209.

41. Richard Hofstadter, *Anti-intellectualism in American Life* (New York: Vintage Books, 1963), 132.

42. AGB to Mabel Gardiner Bell, July 11, 1897, FP.

43. Sara E. Conlon, "Alexander Graham Bell Association for the Deaf," *GEDPD*, 1: 12.

44. Gina Doggett, "Volta Review," *GEDPD*, 3: 336.

45. AGB, "The New Departure Explained," *Volta Review* 12 (April 1910): 7–11.

46. Edward Allen Fay, "Tabular Statement of the Institutions of the Deaf and Dumb of the World," *Annals* 27 (January 1882): 53.

47. Edward Allen Fay, "Progress of Speech-Teaching in the United States," *Annals* 60 (January 1915): 115.

48. H. Van Allen, "A Brief History of the Pennsylvania Institution for the Deaf and Dumb," p. 11, in Fay, ed., *Histories*, vol. 1.

49. Ibid., 20.

50. A. L. E. Crouter, "Recent Changes of Method in the Pennsylvania Institution for the Deaf," published in "The Conference of Principals," *Association Review* 2 (October 1900): 418.

51. Ibid., 418–419.

52. Edward Allen Fay, "Tabular Statement of American Schools for the Deaf, November 10, 1910," *Annals* 56 (January 1911): 20.

53. Van Cleve, "Oral Law," 195.

54. Ibid., 199–200.

55. Ibid., 207.

56. Ibid., 206–207.

57. Ibid., 216.

CHAPTER 11

1. A full explication of Gallaudet's attitude toward sign language and speech is in Thomas H. Gallaudet, "The Natural Language of Signs; and Its Value and Uses in the Instruction of the Deaf and Dumb," *Annals* 1 (October 1847): 55–60, and (January 1848): 79–93.

2. Benjamin D. Pettengill, "The Instruction of the Deaf and Dumb," *Annals* 17 (January 1872): 31.

3. Ibid., 31–32.

4. Ibid., 21–23.

5. Benjamin D. Pettengill, "The Sign Language," *Annals* 18 (January 1873): 5–6.

6. George Wing, "The Associative Feature in the Education of the Deaf," *Annals* 31 (January 1886): 22–23.

7. Jack Gannon, *Deaf Heritage: A Narrative History of Deaf America* (Silver Spring, Md.: National Association of the Deaf, 1981), 170.

8. Robert P. McGregor, "The Social Side of Oralism," *Nebraska Journal* 39 (November 15, 1910): 3.

9. E. S. Tillinghast, "Comments on an Address Given at the Eighth Summer Meeting of the AAPTSD," *Association Review* 11 (October 1909): 350.

10. Judy Mannes, "Olof Hanson," *GEDPD*, 2: 1–3.

11. Olof Hanson to AGB, February 13, 1889, FP.

12. AGB to Sister Mary, January 7, 1898, FP.

13. Quoted in Edward A. Fay, "Nebraska School," *Annals* 56 (May 1911): 347.

14. Olof Hanson to the Governor of Nebraska, February 22, 1911, Hanson Papers, GUA.

15. Edwin A. Hodgson, "Editorial," *Deaf-Mutes' Journal* 40 (May 18, 1911): 2.

16. Frank W. Booth to Olof Hanson, November 9, 1911, Hanson Papers, GUA.

17. "Mississippi," *Deaf-Mutes' Journal* 40 (August 31, 1911): 4; "Kansas Association Convention," *Deaf-Mutes' Journal* 40 (September 14, 1911): 2; "Resolutions," *The Silent Worker* 14 (October 1911): 16.

18. Carrol G. Pearse, "The Oral Teaching of the Deaf," *Nebraska Journal* 40 (January 30, 1912): 2–3.

19. George W. Veditz, "The Nebraska Iniquity," *Deaf-Mutes' Journal* 40 (May 18, 1911): 2.

20. P. L. Axling to Olof Hanson, printed in *Deaf-Mutes' Journal* 42 (January 16, 1913): 2.

21. Olof Hanson to the editors of *Omaha Daily News*, *Omaha Bee*, and *Omaha World-Herald*, December 30, 1912, National Association of the Deaf Collection, GUA.

22. Olof Hanson to J. H. Morehead, January 1, 1913, National Association of the Deaf Collection, GUA.

23. Olof Hanson to William Davis, January 5, 1913, National Association of the Deaf Collection, GUA.

24. Olof Hanson to John H. Grossman, J. M. McFarland, J. M. Talcott, and F. Haarman, February 3, 1913, National Association of the Deaf Collection, GUA.

25. *Nebraska Journal* 43 (1915): 4.

26. Gannon, *Deaf Heritage*, 215.

27. J. Schuyler Long, *The Sign Language: A Manual of Signs*, 2nd ed. (Iowa City, Iowa: Athens Press, 1952), 10.

28. Marina McIntire, "Sign Language Textbooks," *GEDPD*, 3: 27.

29. Quoted in Van Cleve, "George William Veditz," *GEDPD*, 3: 334.

30. John S. Schuchman, "Television and Motion Pictures: The George W. Veditz Film Collection," *GEDPD*, 3: 279–280.

31. Edward Allen Fay, "Illinois Day-Schools," *Annals* 5 (January 1906): 99–100; Gannon, *Deaf Heritage*, 364.

CHAPTER 12

1. Daniel J. Kevles, *In the Name of Eugenics: Genetics and the Uses of Human Heredity* (New York: Alfred A. Knopf, 1985), ix.

2. "List of Pupils of the American Asylum," *Annals* 4 (July 1852): 202–236.

3. Nora Groce, *Everyone Here Spoke Sign Language: Hereditary Deafness on Martha's Vineyard* (Cambridge: Harvard University Press, 1985), 3.

4. Ibid., 22.

5. "List of Pupils," 236.

6. Quoted in *Annals* 13 (March 1861): 33.

7. AGB to Joseph Lee, November 21, 1895, FP.

8. Groce, *Everyone*, 44.

9. Marion P. Downs, "Hearing Loss: Prenatal Causes," *GEDPD*, 2: 23–24; G. R. Fraser, "Hearing Loss: Genetic Causes," *GEDPD*, 2: 20.

10. Most recently reprinted as Alexander Graham Bell, *Memoir upon the Formation of a Deaf Variety of the Human Race* (Washington, D.C.: Alexander Graham Bell Association for the Deaf, 1969).

11. Ibid., 19.

12. Ibid., 4.

13. Ibid., 41.

14. Ibid., 41–45.

15. Sign language writing, known as "mimography," was suggested by George Hutton. See "Posthumous Papers of the Late George Hutton, F.E.I.S.—II," *Annals* 20 (January 1875): 96n.

16. Bell, *Memoir*, 45.

17. Ibid., 46–48.

18. Mabel Gardiner Bell to AGB, June 1, 1898, FP.

19. Michael Anagnos to AGB, October 21, 1883, FP.

20. Michael Katz, *In the Shadow of the Poorhouse: A Social History of Welfare in America* (New York: Basic Books, 1986), 183.

21. R. Mathison to AGB, February 3, 1885, FP; Warring Wilkinson to AGB, January 15, 1885, FP; John W. Swiler to AGB, March 24, 1884, FP; David C. Dudley to AGB, January 14, 1885, FP.

22. Isaac Lewis Peet to AGB, May 8, 1884, FP.

23. Dudley to AGB, January 14, 1885.

24. Peet to AGB, May 8, 1884.

25. AGB to William Henry Brewer, January 27, 1885, FP.

26. James E. Gallaher to AGB, November 24, 1883, FP.

27. James L. Smith, "Clannishness," *Annals* 32 (October 1887): 247.

28. Edward Allen Fay, "Notices of Publications," *Annals* 32 (October 1887): 250–251.

29. Samuel G. Davidson to AGB, December 31, 1884, FP.

30. AGB to Brewer, January 27, 1885.

31. AGB to Mabel Gardiner Bell, June 16, 1885, FP; AGB to Mabel Gardiner Bell, July 17, 1885, FP; AGB to Mabel Gardiner Bell, December 3, 1885, FP; AGB to Mabel Gardiner Bell, December 8, 1885, FP; AGB to Mabel Gardiner Bell, November 13, 1887, FP; AGB to Mabel Gardiner Bell, December 1887, FP; AGB to Mabel Gardiner Bell, June 9, 1888, FP; Richard L. Pease to AGB, August 19, 1888, FP; AGB to Mrs. Richard L. Pease, November 6, 1888, FP.

32. AGB to Mabel Gardiner Bell, June 11, 1888, FP; AGB to Lee, November 21, 1895, FP.

33. Edward Allen Fay, "An Inquiry Concerning the Results of Marriages of the Deaf in America," *Annals* 41 (January 1896): 23.

34. Ibid., 27.

35. Ibid., 22.

36. Edward Allen Fay, "An Inquiry Concerning the Results of Marriages of the Deaf in America. Chapter 1," *Annals* 41 (February 1896): 79.

37. Edward Allen Fay, "An Inquiry Concerning the Results of Marriages of the Deaf in America. Chapter VII," *Annals* 42 (February 1897): 99.

38. Ibid., 100.

39. Ibid., 106.

40. Fraser, "Hearing Loss," 20.

41. Hermine M. Pashayan and Murray Feingold, "Heredity and Deafness," in Larry J. Bradford and William G. Hardy, eds., *Hearing and Hearing Impairment* (New York: Grune and Stratton, 1979), 128.

42. Fraser, "Hearing Loss," 21.

43. Fay, "Inquiry. Chapter VII," 109.

44. AGB, "Open Letter," FP.

45. Hypatia Boyd, *Paul Binner and His Noble Work among the Deaf* (Milwaukee, Wis.: n.p., 1901), 42.

46. Edward Allen Fay, "School Items: Wisconsin," *Annals* 48 (November 1903): 491.

47. Letter, Hypatia Boyd Reed to Frances Wettstein, April 1912. Reprinted in A. J. Winnie, comp., *History and Handbook of Day Schools for the Deaf and Blind* (Madison, Wis.: Democrat Printing Company, 1912), 98–99.

CHAPTER 13

1. Statistics collected by a Chicago deaf club in 1892 present an interesting contrast with those collected by the Kansas Institution for the Deaf in the same year. In Chicago most deaf workers in 1892 were in semi-industrial jobs—printing—whereas in Kansas, still rural, most deaf workers were employed in farming and skilled crafts, especially shoemaking and cabinet-making. "Employments of the Deaf," *Annals* 38 (January 1893): 78–79.

2. Quoted in "Miscellaneous," *Annals* 30 (October 1885): 300.

3. Anson R. Spear is one such example. Barry A. Crouch, "Anson Randolph Spear," *GEDPD*, 3: 190.

4. James L. Smith, "The Deaf and the Civil Service," *Annals* 38 (October 1893): 274–277.

5. John C. Black et al. to Theodore Roosevelt, February 28, 1908. Printed in Edward Allen Fay, "The Deaf and the Civil Service," *Annals* 53 (May 1908): 250–251.

6. Theodore Roosevelt to the Civil Service Commission, printed in ibid., 251.

7. Black et al., in ibid., 251.

8. Ibid., 256.

9. Edward Allen Fay, "The Deaf and the Civil Service," *Annals* 54 (September 1909): 387–389.

10. Edward Allen Fay, "The Eleventh Census—II," *Annals* 43 (November 1898): 353; Edward Allen Fay, "The Twelfth Census of the Deaf of the United States—VI," *Annals* 53 (March 1908): 161.

11. Kathryn P. Meadow-Orlans, "Deaf Population: Deafened Adults," *GEDPD*, 1: 279–283.

12. Warren Robinson, "The Industrial Status of the Deaf," *Annals* 49 (November 1904): 460.

13. Ibid., 461-464.

14. Edward Allen Fay, "Tabular Statement of American Schools for the Deaf," *Annals* 53 (January 1908): 38–39.

15. Warren Robinson, "An Industrial Journal," *Annals* 51 (January 1906): 108.

16. Lucy Taylor, "Dressmaking for Girls," *Annals* 44 (September 1909): 353–355.

17. Robert S. Taylor, "Farming as an Occupation for the Deaf," *Annals* 53 (November 1908): 479–483.

18. Crouch, "Spear," 190.

19. "A Proposed Bureau of Labor," *Annals* 59 (September 1914): 415–417.

20. Michael J. Olson, "Benjamin Marshall Schowe, Sr.," *GEDPD*, 3: 1.

21. Gilbert C. Braddock, "Firestone: The New Silent Colony," *The Silent Worker* 31 (May 1919): 135–136.

22. "Tabular Statement," *Annals* 53 (January 1918): 38-39.

23. John V. Van Cleve, "George William Veditz," *GEDPD*, 3: 333; John V. Van Cleve, "Little Paper Family," *GEDPD*, 2: 194.

24. Jerome Schein, "Frederick Carl Schreiber," *GEDPD*, 3: 3.

25. Van Cleve, "Veditz," 333.

26. Jack Gannon, *Deaf Heritage: A Narrative History of Deaf America* (Silver Spring, Md.: National Association of the Deaf, 1981), 16, 65.

27. James E. Gallagher [*sic*], "Deaf-Mutes as Printers," *Annals* 25 (April 1880): 135.

28. U.S. Bureau of the Census, *Historical Statistics of the United States, Colonial Times to 1970, Bicentennial Edition*, pt. 1 (Washington, D.C.: Government Printing Office, 1975)*,* 165.

29. Odie W. Underhill, "The Deaf Man and the Printing Trades," *Annals* 68 (September 1923): 326.

CHAPTER 14

1. For a discussion of the characteristics of leaders of American ethnic groups, see John Higham, ed., *Ethnic Leadership in America* (Baltimore, Md.: Johns Hopkins University Press, 1978).

2. Elaine Gardner, "Driving Restrictions," *GEDPD*, 1: 306–308.

3. See, for example, Sarah Geer and Mary-Jean Sweeney, "Rehabilitation Act of 1973," *GEDPD*, 2: 407–412; Sy DuBow, "Rehabilitation Act of 1973: Southeastern Community College v. Davis," *GEDPD*, 2: 412–414; and Charles M. Firestone, "Rehabilitation Act of 1973: Gottfried v. Community Television of Southern California." *GEDPD*, 2: 416–420.

4. Sarah S. Geer, "Education of the Handicapped Act," *GEDPD*, 1: 380–382.

5. Unless otherwise noted, the DPN events described herein were personally witnessed by one or both of the authors.

6. Gallaudet University Student Body Press Release, n.d.

7. "Elisabeth Zinser, in Conclusion," *Washington Post*, March 12, 1988, p. C-9.

8. Gallaudet University Office of Public Relations, Press Release, March 13, 1988.

Bibliography

MANUSCRIPT COLLECTIONS

Alexander Graham Bell Family Papers. Manuscript Division, Library of Congress, Washington, D.C.

Archives of the American School for the Deaf. American School for the Deaf, West Hartford, Connecticut.

William Albert Bolling. William Albert Bolling Manuscript School Book. Volta Bureau, Washington, D.C.

William Bolling. William Bolling Letterbook. Valentine Museum, Richmond, Virginia.

Bolling Family Papers. William R. Perkins Library, Duke University, Durham, North Carolina.

Laurent Clerc Papers. Sterling Memorial Library, Yale University, New Haven, Connecticut.

Mason Fitch Cogswell Collection. Beineke Memorial Library, Yale University, New Haven, Connecticut.

Thomas Hopkins Gallaudet Collection. Manuscript Division, Library of Congress, Washington, D.C.

Olof Hanson Papers. Gallaudet University Archives, Gallaudet University, Washington, D.C.

National Association of the Deaf Collection. Gallaudet University Archives, Gallaudet University, Washington, D.C.

Tillinghast Family Papers. William R. Perkins Library, Duke University, Durham, North Carolina.

PUBLISHED MATERIALS

Axling, P. L. Letter to Olof Hanson. Printed in *Deaf-Mutes' Journal* 42 (January 16, 1913): 2.

Baker-Shenk, Charlotte. "Sign Languages: Facial Expressions." *Gallaudet Encyclopedia of Deaf People and Deafness* 3: 37–43. *See* Van Cleve, ed.

Barnard, Henry. "Thomas Hopkins Gallaudet: Eulogy." *American Annals of the Deaf* 4 (January 1852): 81–136.

"Beer and Tobacco." *The Silent Worker* 2 (December 20, 1888): 1.

Bell, Alexander Graham. "Fallacies Concerning the Deaf." *American Annals of the Deaf* 29 (January 1884): 32–60.

———. "Historical Notes Concerning the Teaching of Speech to the Deaf." *Association Review* 2 (February 1900): 33–68.

———. *Memoir upon the Formation of a Deaf Variety of the Human Race.* Washington, D.C.: Government Printing Office, 1884; reissued by Alexander Graham Bell Association for the Deaf, 1969.

———. "The New Departure Explained." *Volta Review* 12 (April 1910): 7–11.

Bernard, Rene. "Abbé Charles Michel de l'Épée." *Gallaudet Encyclopedia of Deaf People and Deafness* 1: 416–418. *See* Van Cleve, ed.

Best, Harry. *Deafness and the Deaf in the United States.* New York: Macmillan, 1943.

Boatner, Maxine Tull. *Voice of the Deaf: A Biography of Edward Miner Gallaudet.* Washington, D.C.: Public Affairs Press, 1959.

Booth, Edmund. *Edmund Booth, Forty-Niner.* Stockton, Calif.: San Joaquin Pioneer and Historical Society, 1953.

———. Letter to J. J. Flournoy in "Mr. Flournoy's Plan for a Deaf-Mute Commonwealth." *American Annals of the Deaf* 10 (January 1858): 40–42.

———. "Rev. Joseph Dennis Tyler." *American Era* 31 (January 1945): 37–39.

Boyd, Hypatia. *Paul Binner and His Noble Work Among the Deaf.* Milwaukee, Wis.: n.p., 1901.

Braddock, Gilbert C. "Firestone: The New Silent Colony." *The Silent Worker* 31 (May 1919): 135–136.

Bradford, Larry J., and Hardy, William G., eds. *Hearing and Hearing Impairment.* New York: Grune and Stratton, 1979.

Bringhurst, Newell G. *Brigham Young and the Expanding American Frontier.* Boston: Little Brown, 1986.

Bruce, Robert V. *Bell: Alexander Graham Bell and the Conquest of Solitude.* Boston: Little, Brown, 1973.

Bullard, Douglas. *Islay.* Silver Spring, Md.: T. J. Publishers, 1986.

Bulwer, John. *Philocophus, or, the deaf and dumbe man's friend. . . .* London: H. Moseley, 1648.

Carlin, John. "Advantages and Disadvantages of the Use of Signs." *American Annals of the Deaf* 4 (October 1851): 49–57.

———. "The National College for Mutes." *American Annals of the Deaf* 6 (April 1854): 175–183.

———. "Oration: A College for the Deaf and Dumb." In *Seventh Annual Report of the Columbia Institution for the Deaf and Dumb and the Blind*. Washington, D.C.: n.p., 1864.

Chamberlain, William. "Mr. Chamberlain and others on Mr. Flournoy's Project." *American Annals of the Deaf* 10 (April 1858): 84–87.

———. "Proceedings of the Board of Managers of the 'New England Gallaudet Association of Deaf-Mutes.'" *American Annals of the Deaf* 11 (October 1859): 210–216.

———. "Proceedings of the Convention of the New England Gallaudet Association of Deaf-Mutes." *American Annals of the Deaf* 9 (April 1857): 65–87.

———. "Proceedings of the Third Convention of the New England Gallaudet Association of Deaf-Mutes." *American Annals of the Deaf* 10 (October 1858): 205–219.

Chasin, Werner D. "The Clinical Management of Otologic Disorders." In *Hearing and Hearing Impairment*, 93–108. See Bradford and Hardy, eds.

Confer, P. H. Letter to Samuel Porter in "Mr. Chamberlain and Others on Mr. Flournoy's Project." *American Annals of the Deaf* 10 (April 1858): 87–88.

Conlon, Sara E. "Alexander Graham Bell Association for the Deaf." *Gallaudet Encyclopedia of Deaf People and Deafness* 1: 12–14. See Van Cleve, ed.

Crouch, Barry A. "Alienation and the Mid-Nineteenth Century American Deaf Community: A Response." *American Annals of the Deaf* 131 (December 1986): 322–324.

———. "Anson Randolph Spear." *Gallaudet Encyclopedia of Deaf People and Deafness* 3: 190–191. See Van Cleve, ed.

Crouter, A. L. E. "Recent Changes of Method in the Pennsylvania Institution for the Deaf." In "The Conference of Principals." *Association Review* 2 (October 1900): 418–419.

Currier, E. H., and Fox, Thomas. "New York Institution for the Instruction of the Deaf and Dumb." In *Histories of American Schools for the Deaf, 1817–1893*, vol. 1. See Fay, ed.

de Lorenzo, David. "Edward Miner Gallaudet." *Gallaudet Encyclopedia of Deaf People and Deafness* 1: 439–444. See Van Cleve, ed.

Denis, Taras B. "James Nack." *Gallaudet Encyclopedia of Deaf People and Deafness* 2: 119–120. See Van Cleve, ed.

Digby, Kenelm. *Of Bodies, and of Man's Soul*. London: John Williams, 1669.

Doggett, Gina. "Volta Review." *Gallaudet Encyclopedia of Deaf People and Deafness* 3: 336. See Van Cleve, ed.

Downs, Marion P. "Hearing Loss: Prenatal Causes." *Gallaudet Encyclopedia of Deaf People and Deafness* 2: 23–24. See Van Cleve, ed.

Doyle, Thomas S. "The Virginia Institution for the Education of the Deaf and Dumb (and of the Blind)." In *Histories of American Schools for the Deaf, 1817–1893*, vol. 1. See Fay, ed.

DuBow, Sy. "Rehabilitation Act of 1973: Southeastern Community College v. Davis." *Gallaudet Encyclopedia of Deaf People and Deafness* 2: 412–414. *See* Van Cleve, ed.

"Employments of the Deaf." *American Annals of the Deaf* 38 (January 1893): 78–79.

Fay, Edward Allen. "Day Schools." *American Annals of the Deaf* 44 (September 1899): 395–396.

———. "Day Schools in California." *American Annals of the Deaf* 48 (May 1903): 304.

———. "Day-Schools in Wisconsin." *American Annals of the Deaf* 30 (October 1885): 302.

———. "The Deaf and the Civil Service." *American Annals of the Deaf* 53 (May 1908): 249–256.

———. "The Deaf and the Civil Service." *American Annals of the Deaf* 54 (September 1909): 387–389.

———. "The Eleventh Census—II." *American Annals of the Deaf* 43 (November 1898): 345–359.

———. "Illinois Day-Schools." *American Annals of the Deaf* 51 (January 1906): 99–100.

———."An Inquiry Concerning the Results of Marriages of the Deaf in America." *American Annals of the Deaf* 41 (January 1896): 22–31.

———. "An Inquiry Concerning the Results of Marriages of the Deaf in America. Chapter 1." *American Annals of the Deaf* 41 (February 1896): 79–88.

———. "An Inquiry Concerning the Results of Marriages of the Deaf in America. Chapter VII." *American Annals of the Deaf* 42 (February 1897): 96–109.

———. "Nebraska School." *American Annals of the Deaf* 56 (May 1911): 347–348.

———. "Notices of Publications." *American Annals of the Deaf* 32 (October 1887): 250–251.

———. "Progress of Speech-Teaching in the United States." *American Annals of the Deaf* 60 (January 1915): 115.

———. "School Items: Wisconsin." *American Annals of the Deaf* 48 (November 1903): 491.

———. "Tabular Statement of American Schools for the Deaf." *American Annals of the Deaf* 53 (January 1908): 36–52.

———. "Tabular Statement of American Schools for the Deaf, November 10, 1910." *American Annals of the Deaf* 56 (January 1911): 18–26.

———. "Tabular Statement of the Institutions of the Deaf and Dumb of the World." *American Annals of the Deaf* 27 (January 1882): 32–53.

———. "The Twelfth Census of the Deaf of the United States—VI." *American Annals of the Deaf* 53 (March 1908): 159–172.

———. "What did St. Augustine Say?" *American Annals of the Deaf* 57 (January 1912): 108–120.

———, ed. *Histories of American Schools for the Deaf, 1817–1893.* 3 vols. Washington, D.C.: Volta Bureau, 1893.

Fernandes, James J. "Thomas Hopkins Gallaudet. *Gallaudet Encyclopedia of Deaf People and Deafness.*" 1: 444–447. *See* Van Cleve, ed.

Firestone, Charles M. "Rehabilitation Act of 1973: Gottfried v. Community Television of Southern California." *Gallaudet Encyclopedia of Deaf People and Deafness* 2: 416–420. *See* Van Cleve, ed.

Fischer, Angelina Fuller. "Edmund Booth." In *Representative Deaf Persons of the United States of America*, 11–16. *See* Gallaher, ed.

Frankenheim, Samuel. "History of the Deaf-Mutes' Union League." *Deaf-Mutes' Journal* 35 (January 11, 1906): 1.

Fraser, G. R. "Hearing Loss: Genetic Causes." *Gallaudet Encyclopedia of Deaf People and Deafness* 2: 2–23. *See* Van Cleve, ed.

Froehlich, Theodore A. "Importance of Association among Mutes for Mutual Improvement." *Proceedings of the First National Convention of Deaf-Mutes.* New York: New York Institution for the Deaf and Dumb, 1880.

A Future for the Deaf and Dumb in the Canadian North-West. London: Potter Brothers, 1884.

Gallaher, James E. "Deaf-Mutes as Printers." *American Annals of the Deaf* 25 (April 1880): 134–135.

——, ed. *Representative Deaf Persons of the United States of America.* Chicago: James E. Gallaher, 1898.

Gallaudet, Edward Miner. "The American System of Deaf-Mute Instruction—Its Incidental Defects and Their Remedies." *American Annals of the Deaf* 13 (September 1868): 147–171.

——. "The Columbia Institution for the Instruction of the Deaf and Dumb." In *Histories of American Schools for the Deaf, 1817–1893*, vol. 2. *See* Fay, ed.

——. *Eighth Annual Report of the Columbia Institution for the Deaf and Dumb.* Washington, D.C.: n.p., 1865.

——. *History of the College for the Deaf, 1857–1907.* Edited by Lance J. Fischer and David de Lorenzo. Washington, D.C.: Gallaudet College Press, 1983.

——. "The Milan Convention." *American Annals of the Deaf* 26 (January 1881): 1–16.

Gallaudet, Thomas Hopkins. "The Natural Language of Signs; and Its Value and Uses in the Instruction of the Deaf and Dumb." *American Annals of the Deaf* 1 (October 1847): 55–60; and (January 1848): 79–93.

——. *Sermon on the Duty and Advantages of Affording Instruction to the Deaf and Dumb.* Concord, Mass.: Isaac Hill, 1824.

Gallaudet, Thomas Hopkins, and Clerc, Laurent. "Contract Between Gallaudet and Clerc, 1816." *American Annals of the Deaf* 24 (April 1879): 115–117.

Gannon, Jack. *Deaf Heritage: A Narrative History of Deaf America.* Silver Spring, Md.: National Association of the Deaf, 1981.

Gardner, Elaine. "Driving Restrictions." *Gallaudet Encyclopedia of Deaf People and Deafness* 1: 306–308. *See* Van Cleve, ed.

Geer, Sarah S. "Education of the Handicapped Act." *Gallaudet Encyclopedia of Deaf People and Deafness* 1: 380–382. *See* Van Cleve, ed.

Geer, Sarah S., and Sweeney, Mary-Jean. "Rehabilitation Act of 1973." *Gallaudet Encyclopedia of Deaf People and Deafness* 2: 407–412. *See* Van Cleve, ed.

Gillett, Philip. "Dr. Gillett to Mr. Bell." *The Silent Worker* 4 (November 27, 1890): 1–4.

Goodwin, D. McK. "The North Carolina Institution for the Deaf and Dumb and Blind." In *Histories of American Schools for the Deaf, 1817–1893*. vol. 1. *See* Fay, ed.

Green, David. "The Institution for the Improved Instruction of Deaf-Mutes." In *Histories of American Schools for the Deaf, 1817–1893*, vol. 2. *See* Fay, ed.

Green, Samuel. "The Earliest Advocate of the Education of Deaf-Mutes in America." *American Annals of the Deaf* 13 (March 1861): 1–7.

Groce, Nora. *Everyone Here Spoke Sign Language: Hereditary Deafness on Martha's Vineyard.* Cambridge: Harvard University Press, 1985.

Harmon, Robert. "Samuel Heinicke." *Gallaudet Encyclopedia of Deaf People and Deafness* 2: 35–38. *See* Van Cleve, ed.

Harrower, John. "Documents: Diary of John Harrower, 1773–1776." *American Historical Review* 6 (October 1900): 65–107.

Higgins, Francis C. "John Carlin." *Gallaudet Encyclopedia of Deaf People and Deafness* 1: 178–179. *See* Van Cleve, ed.

———. "John Kitto." *Gallaudet Encyclopedia of Deaf People and Deafness* 2: 129–131. *See* Van Cleve, ed.

Higgins, Paul C. *Outsiders in a Hearing World: A Sociology of Deafness.* Beverly Hills, Calif.: Sage Publications, 1980.

Higham, John, ed. *Ethnic Leadership in America.* Baltimore, Md.: Johns Hopkins University Press, 1978.

Hodgson, Edwin A. "Editorial." *Deaf-Mutes' Journal* 40 (May 18, 1911): 2.

Hofstadter, Richard. *Anti-intellectualism in American Life.* New York: Vintage Books, 1963.

"How to Teach Deaf Mutes." *Philadelphia Sun*, June 29, 1896.

Hutton, George. "Posthumous Papers of the Late George Hutton, F.E.I.S.—II." *American Annals of the Deaf* 20 (January 1875): 91–99.

"Intermarriage Again." *The Silent Worker* 27 (December 25, 1890): 1.

Jefferson, Thomas, and Cabbell, Joseph C. *Early History of the University of Virginia, as Contained in the Letters of Thomas Jefferson and Joseph C. Cabbell.* Richmond, Va.: J. W. Randolph, 1856.

Katz, Michael. *In the Shadow of the Poorhouse: A Social History of Welfare in America.* New York: Basic Books, 1986.

Kevles, Daniel J. *In the Name of Eugenics: Genetics and the Uses of Human Heredity.* New York: Alfred A. Knopf, 1985.

Klopfer, Stephen. *St. Augustine and the Deaf.* Columbus, Ohio: Catholic Educational Association, n.d.

Lane, Harlan. *When the Mind Hears: A History of the Deaf.* New York: Random House, 1984.

——, ed. *The Deaf Experience: Classics in Language and Education.* Translated by Franklin Philip. Cambridge: Harvard University Press, 1984.

"List of Pupils of the American Asylum." *American Annals of the Deaf* 4 (July 1852): 202–236.

Little, Nina Fletcher. "John Brewster, Jr." *Gallaudet Encyclopedia of Deaf People and Deafness* 1: 156–157.

Long, J. Schuyler. *The Sign Language: A Manual of Signs.* 2nd ed. Iowa City, Iowa: Athens Press, 1952.

McGregor, Robert P. "The Social Side of Oralism." *Nebraska Journal* 39 (November 15, 1910): 3.

McIntire, Marina. "Sign Language Textbooks." *Gallaudet Encyclopedia of Deaf People and Deafness* 3: 26–29. See Van Cleve, ed.

"The Manitoba Colonists." *American Annals of the Deaf* 31 (July 1886): 228.

Mannes, Judy. "Olof Hanson." *Gallaudet Encyclopedia of Deaf People and Deafness* 2: 1–3. See Van Cleve, ed.

Mattingly, Paul H. "History: Deafness and Reform." *Gallaudet Encyclopedia of Deaf People and Deafness* 2: 45–52. See Van Cleve, ed.

Meadow-Orlans, Kathryn P. "Deaf Population: Deafened Adults." *Gallaudet Encyclopedia of Deaf People and Deafness* 1: 279–283. See Van Cleve, ed.

Merrill, Edward C., Jr. "Gallaudet College." *Gallaudet Encyclopedia of Deaf People and Deafness* 1: 447–454. See Van Cleve, ed.

Miller, Perry. *Errand into the Wilderness.* New York: Harper and Row, 1956.

"Miscellaneous." *American Annals of the Deaf* 30 (October 1885): 300.

"Mississippi." *Deaf-Mutes' Journal* 40 (August 31, 1911): 4.

Moody, William. "Jean-Ferdinand Berthier." *Gallaudet Encyclopedia of Deaf People and Deafness* 1: 141–143. See Van Cleve, ed.

Moores, Donald F. *Educating the Deaf: Psychology, Principles, and Practices.* Boston: Houghton Mifflin, 1982.

Morison, Samuel Eliot. *The Oxford History of the American People.* New York: Oxford University Press, 1965.

Nesbit, Robert. *Wisconsin: A History.* Madison, Wis.: University of Wisconsin Press, 1973.

"Notices of Publications." *American Annals of the Deaf* 31 (January 1886): 63–64.

Olson, Michael J. "Benjamin Marshall Schowe, Sr." *Gallaudet Encyclopedia of Deaf People and Deafness* 3: 1–3. See Van Cleve, ed.

O'Neill, Ynez Viole. *Speech and Speech Disorders in Western Thought Before 1600.* Westport, Conn.: Greenwood Press, 1980.

Pablo Bonet, Juan. *Simplification of the Letters of the Alphabet and Method of Teaching Deaf-Mutes to Speak.* Translated by H. N. Dixon. London: Hazell, Watson, and Viney, 1890.

Pashayan, Hermine M., and Feingold, Murray. "Heredity and Deafness." In *Hearing and Hearing Impairment,* 125–144. See Bradford and Hardy, eds.

Pearse, Carrol G. "The Oral Teaching of the Deaf." *Nebraska Journal* 40 (January 30, 1912): 2–3.

Peet, Harvey P. "Memoir on the Origin and Early History of the Art of Instructing the Deaf and Dumb." *American Annals of the Deaf* 3 (April 1851): 129–160.

Pettengill, Benjamin D. "The Instruction of the Deaf and Dumb." *American Annals of the Deaf* 17 (January 1872): 21–33.

———. "The Sign Language." *American Annals of the Deaf* 18 (January 1873): 1–12.

"A Proposed Bureau of Labor." *American Annals of the Deaf* 59 (September 1914): 415–417.

Redkey, Edwin S. *Black Exodus: Black Nationalist and Back-to-Africa Movements, 1890–1910.* New Haven, Conn.: Yale University Press, 1969.

Reed, Hypatia Boyd. Letter to Frances Wettstein. In *History and Handbook of Day Schools for the Deaf and Blind,* 98–99. See Winnie, comp.

Remini, Robert V. *Andrew Jackson and the Course of American Freedom, 1822–1832.* New York: Harper and Row, 1981.

"Resolutions." *The Silent Worker* 24 (October 1911): 16.

Rider, H. C. "Elmira Convention of Deaf Mutes." *American Annals of the Deaf* 22 (October 1877): 251–252.

Robertson, Wyndham, and Brook, R. A. *Pocahontas, Alias Matoaka, and Her Descendants.* Baltimore, Md.: Genealogical Publishing Company, 1982.

Robinson, Warren. "An Industrial Journal." *American Annals of the Deaf* 51 (January 1906): 108–109.

———. "The Industrial Status of the Deaf." *American Annals of the Deaf* 49 (November 1904): 460–464.

Root, Grace Cogswell, ed. *Father and Daughter: A Collection of Cogswell Family Letters and Diaries.* West Hartford, Conn.: American School for the Deaf, 1924.

Saegert, C. W. "Education of the Deaf and Dumb in Prussia." Translated by Benjamin Talbot. *American Annals of the Deaf* 9 (October 1857): 193–220.

Sanborn, F. B. "The Clarke Institution for Deaf Mutes." In *Histories of American Schools for the Deaf, 1817–1893,* vol. 2. See Fay, ed.

Schein, Jerome. "National Association of the Deaf." *Gallaudet Encyclopedia of Deaf People and Deafness* 2: 220–221. See Van Cleve, ed.

———. "Frederick Carl Schreiber." *Gallaudet Encyclopedia of Deaf People and Deafness* 3: 3–5. See Van Cleve, ed.

"Schools and Classes for the Deaf in the United States." *American Annals of the Deaf* 130 (April 1985): 81–129.

Schuchman, John S. "Television and Motion Pictures: The George W. Veditz Film Collection." *Gallaudet Encyclopedia of Deaf People and Deafness* 3: 279–281. See Van Cleve, ed.

Sibscota, George, trans. *The Deaf and Dumb Man's Discourse,* by Anthony Deusing. London: William Crook, 1670.

Smith, James L. "Clannishness." *American Annals of the Deaf* 32 (October 1887): 246–250.

——. "The Deaf and the Civil Service." *American Annals of the Deaf* 38 (October 1893): 274–277.

Spencer, Robert C. "The Wisconsin System of Public Day Schools." In *Histories of American Schools for the Deaf, 1817–1893*, vol. 3. *See* Fay, ed.

Sullivan, Frank B. "National Fraternal Society of the Deaf." *Gallaudet Encyclopedia of Deaf People and Deafness* 2: 224–227. *See* Van Cleve, ed.

"Tabular Statement of American Schools for the Deaf." *American Annals of the Deaf* 63 (January 1918): 48–67.

"Tabular Statement of American Schools for the Deaf, October 20, 1920." *American Annals of the Deaf* 66 (January 1921): 34–53.

Taylor, Lucy. "Dressmaking for Girls." *American Annals of the Deaf* 44 (September 1909): 353–355.

Taylor, Robert S. "Farming as an Occupation for the Deaf." *American Annals of the Deaf* 53 (November 1908): 479–483.

Terry, Seth. *Third Report of the Directors of the Connecticut Asylum for the Education and Instruction of Deaf and Dumb Persons.* Hartford, Conn.: Hudson and Company, 1819.

"David Ray Tillinghast." In *Representative Deaf Persons of the United States of America,* 180–181. *See* Gallaher, ed.

Tillinghast, E. S. "Comments on an Address Given at the Eighth Summer Meeting of the AAPTSD." *Association Review* 11 (October 1909): 347–352.

Turner, William W. "Laurent Clerc." *American Annals of the Deaf* 15 (January 1870): 16–25.

——. Letter to J. J. Flournoy in "Scheme for a Commonwealth." *American Annals of the Deaf* 8 (January 1856): 118–120.

Underhill, Odie W. "The Deaf Man and the Printing Trades." *American Annals of the Deaf* 68 (September 1923): 317–330.

U.S. Bureau of the Census. *Historical Statistics of the United States, Colonial Times to 1970, Bicentennial Edition.* Pt. 1. Washington, D.C.: Government Printing Office, 1975.

Van Allen, H. "A Brief History of the Pennsylvania Institution for the Deaf and Dumb." In *Histories of American Schools for the Deaf, 1817–1893*, vol. 1. *See* Fay, ed.

Van Cleve, John V. "Edmund Booth." *Gallaudet Encyclopedia of Deaf People and Deafness* 1: 143–144. *See* Van Cleve, ed.

——. "Edward Allen Fay." *Gallaudet Encyclopedia of Deaf People and Deafness* 1: 426–428. *See* Van Cleve, ed.

——. "History: Congress of Milan." *Gallaudet Encyclopedia of Deaf People and Deafness* 2: 63–68. *See* Van Cleve, ed.

——. "Little Paper Family." *Gallaudet Encyclopedia of Deaf People and Deafness* 2: 193–195. *See* Van Cleve, ed.

——. "Nebraska's Oral Law of 1911 and the Deaf Community." *Nebraska History* 65 (Summer 1984): 195–220.

——. "George William Veditz." *Gallaudet Encyclopedia of Deaf People and Deafness* 3: 333–335. *See* Van Cleve, ed.

——, ed. *Gallaudet Encyclopedia of Deaf People and Deafness*. 3 volumes. New York: McGraw-Hill Book Company, 1987.

Van Nostrand, Jacob. "Necessity of a Higher Standard of Education for the Deaf and Dumb." *American Annals of the Deaf* 3 (July 1851): 193–198.

Veditz, George W. "The Nebraska Iniquity." *Deaf-Mutes' Journal* 40 (May 18, 1911): 2.

Wadsworth, Daniel; Ely, William; and Hudson, Henry. *First Report of the Connecticut Asylum for the Education and Instruction of Deaf and Dumb Persons*. Hartford, Conn.: n.p., 1817.

Weld, Lewis. "The American Asylum." *American Annals of the Deaf* 1 (January 1848): 93–112.

Werner, Hans. *History of the Problem of Deaf-Mutism until the Seventeenth Century*. Translated by C. K. Bonning. Jena: n.p., 1932.

Wesley, Edgar B. *NEA: The First Hundred Years*. New York: Harper and Brothers, 1957.

Williams, Job. "A Brief History of the American Asylum at Hartford for the Education and Instruction of the Deaf and Dumb." In *Histories of American Schools for the Deaf, 1817–1893*, vol. 1. *See* Fay, ed.

Williams, Melanie Yeager. "Alice Cogswell." *Gallaudet Encyclopedia of Deaf People and Deafness* 1: 196–197. *See* Van Cleve, ed.

Wing, George. "The Associative Feature in the Education of the Deaf." *American Annals of the Deaf* 31 (January 1886): 22–35.

Winnie, A. J., comp. *History and Handbook of Day Schools for the Deaf and Blind*. Madison, Wis.: Democrat Printing Company, 1912.

Winzer, Margaret. "Deaf-Mutia: Responses to Alienation by the Deaf in Mid-Nineteenth Century America." *American Annals of the Deaf* 131 (March 1986): 29–32.

Zillman, Felix. *Saint Augustine and the Education of the Deaf*. Translated by S. Klopfer. Reprint from *Our Young People—the Deaf-Mutes' Friend*, 41: 11–12 and 42: 1–3.

"Elisabeth Zinser, in Conclusion." *Washington Post*, March 12, 1988, p. C-9.

Index

A

Alberti, Solomon, 8
Alexander Graham Bell Association for the Deaf, 154.
See also American Association to Promote the Teaching of Speech to the Deaf
Alexander of Tralles, 6
American Annals of the Deaf, 68, 135
American Association to Promote the Teaching of Speech to the Deaf (AAPTSD), 121–122, 126–127
American School for the Deaf
A. G. Bell and, 116
communication methods in, 30, 44–45
competition with the New York School for the Deaf, 43
funding of, 30, 31, 32, 42–43
importance of religious instruction in, 46
influence of, 29–30, 47
opening of, 29
reasons for success of, 28, 45–46
records of heredity and deafness of, 143
sign language and, 111

American Sign Language, 106
origins of, 45
origins of manual alphabet of, 12
See also Sign language
Anagnos, Michael, 148
Arms, Hiram Phelps, 149
Association Review, 122, 127, 135
Augustine of Hippo, Saint, 4–6
Axling, Philip, 160
Ayres, Jared A., 79

B

Bachrach, Arthur, 96
Bell, Alexander Graham
American Association to Promote the Teaching of Speech to the Deaf and, 121
attitude of, toward the deaf community, 145
day schools and, 117–119
fingerspelling in public schools and, 135
Memoir upon the Formation of a Deaf Variety of the Human Race, 142, 146, 148, 153–154
National Education Association and, 120

203